Céleste perrino Walker

Making Sabbath Special

Simple Traditions to Make the Sabbath a Delight

Pacific Press® Publishing Association
Nampa, Idaho
Oshawa, Ontario, Canada

Edited By Jerry D. Thomas
Designed by Dennis Ferree
Cover photo by Stan Sinclair

Copyright © 1999 by
Pacific Press® Publishing Association
Printed in the United States of America
All Rights Reserved

Library of Congress Cataloging-in Publication Data
Walker, Céleste perrino.
    Making sabbath special : simple traditions to make the day a delight /
Céleste perrino Walker.
        p. cm.
    Includes bibliographical references.
    ISBN 0-8163-1706-2 (alk. paper)
    1. Sabbath. 2. Seventh-day Adventists—Doctrines. I. Title.
BX6154.W324 1999
263'.2—dc21   98-45168
                                                                    CIP

99 00 01 02 03 • 5 4 3 2 1

Contents

Dedication

This book is dedicated with love
to
Sandy and Andy Cheney
Who knew me when . . . and like me anyway.
I love you guys!
And also for their kids: Ashley, Aaron, Hannah, and Leah.

Acknowledgments

In the writing of this book I am indebted to the following people:

Tsevyah, Ehud, Nahara and Yonadab, Qesheth, Debbie, Lev, Shuva-El, and all my other friends at The Community who are now too numerous to name individually, for sharing the Sabbath with me.

Rabbi Solomon Goldberg for patiently teaching me the traditions and celebrations of the Sabbath and its roots.

My friends Jennifer Jill Schwirzer, Kim Johnson, Paula Shaw, and Baird Barsumian for reading the manuscript and giving not only keen insight but kind wisdom, loads of encouragement, and many suggestions. Thank you all.

Preface

I would like to say that this book reflects every aspect of my family's Sabbath celebration. I would like to say that it grew out of our own Sabbath experience. I would like to say that if you stopped by our home on any Friday evening as the sun began to sink into the embrace of the mountains, that you would have an experience typical of what I will be writing about.

I would like to say that.

But, I can't.

Since becoming a Seventh-day Adventist thirteen years ago, I have learned a great deal about the Sabbath. Some of it has been incorrect. Some of it has even been legalistic. But some of it has been enriching. I have tried to keep the good things, improve on the mediocre things, and "observe the Sabbath, because it is holy" (Exodus 31:14*).

But, that has never seemed enough.

No matter how hard I "observed" the Sabbath, it never seemed quite right. It never seemed as much as it *could* be. But I have seen glimpses of what it could be like. I recall a scene from **Fiddler on the Roof** of a Jewish family scurrying to get ready for Sabbath. But as the darkness descended and the candles were lighted, they welcomed God to their Shabbat table as a long-awaited friend, an honored guest. The thought of that scene still makes me wistful.

Vermont is not such a large place that a Messianic community who keep Sabbath and have strong family values can go completely unnoticed. In fact, the entire Sunday section of the newspaper was once devoted to this "strange" group. They call themselves The Community, and they welcome the Sabbath with dinner. All are invited. This is followed by fellowship, testimony, Israeli dances, and singing. These people don't "observe" the Sabbath. They don't "endure" the Sabbath. They CELEBRATE it. They make Sabbath special.

And that is what I'd like to do. Ultimately, the Sabbath is a personal experience, but when you belong to a family, there are other dynamics you must work with in order to create a Sabbath experience that everyone can relate to and celebrate. Throughout this book I will offer suggestions, relay experiences, and, hopefully, give insight into what makes a celebration and what, particularly, makes Sabbath a celebration. I would also like to discuss what hinders a Sabbath celebration.

This book is more a journey than an authority. Won't you walk with me?

---

* Unless otherwise indicated, all texts are from the NIV.

Prologue

The traveler quickened his steps in eager anticipation. A healthy glow radiated from his rugged face. Black hair, peppered with gray and swept back from a high forehead cast shadows on his prominent cheekbones. He walked with an easy, natural stride. It had been a long, tiring week, but soon he would be with his friends again. The thought blocked the fatigue, disappointments, and frustrations of the week and buoyed his spirits as he walked.

The houses ahead, clustered together as if for warmth, seemed strangely silent and inactive. In the first, not one light shone, and no cars were parked in the driveway. Pushing aside a rising feeling of disquiet, the traveler pressed on to the next house. Two boys played ball on the front lawn and did not even seem to notice him as he made his way up the front walk and knocked on the door. A woman answered, her hands covered with flour.

"You're early," she snapped and then glanced past him toward the darkening sky as she flicked little balls of sticky dough from her fingers. "No, I guess I'm late again," she sighed. "You'd think I'd learn eventually, wouldn't you? Look, I'm sorry, but I won't be finished cooking for at least a half hour, and the boys haven't had their baths yet. And the house is a mess. . . ." Her voice trailed off. "It's just been such a busy week. You understand, don't you? Could you come back a little later?"

The traveler nodded sadly and gave his friend's shoulder a gentle squeeze before he pressed on to the next house. The loud blare of the television greeted him through the open window, and it was a long time before his knock was even noticed.

A man answered, still in the clothes he had worn home from the office, his tie loosened around his neck. He seemed surprised to find someone on his doorstep. "Oh, hey there! It must be later than I thought. The game's almost over. It's run into overtime, and I just have to see who wins. It shouldn't be long now. A few minutes more. Would you like to come in and . . . no, I don't suppose you would. Well, like I said, it'll only be another few minutes. You'll come back later, won't you?"

The traveler nodded his assent, but his shoulders drooped and tears of loneliness collected in his frank blue eyes. "Yes," he whispered. "I'll come back."

Feet dragging, he made his way to the next house. Hope revived when he saw nearly every light on and extra cars in the driveway. At last, friends who were expecting him. He nearly bounded up the front steps.

A man answered his knock, and when he saw who stood on the step, his face flushed with embarrassment. "Oh, hi. We've got, uh, company. They're not your type, though, but you're welcome to stay," he added hastily; then he dropped his eyes to the ground. "But you probably wouldn't be comfortable with the way the conversation is going. In fact, I'm not. But what can I do? Kick them out?" He dropped his voice and stepped out of the house, closer to the traveler, partially closing the door behind him. "Can you come back after they've left? There's something I need to talk to you about."

The traveler nodded, his heart heavy. As he turned away, he heard a woman's voice from inside call, "Who's there, honey?"

"Nobody," was the reply, before the door closed and the raucous sounds of laughter were muted.

Only one house remained, and the traveler approached it with a mixture of fear and anticipation. Loneliness throbbed deeply within his chest, and he longed to spend some time with people he loved. Hesitantly he knocked on the door, waiting breathlessly before it was thrown open.

"There you are!" a woman exclaimed. "We thought you'd never get here. Oh, I know you're right on time, but we're always so anxious to see you! Come on in, dinner will get cold if we stand here yammering. Sit right down here at the head of the table. Jeff, you're over there. I'll sit here. Ellen, sit beside your father and Nathan beside me." She looked up expectantly. "Would you have the blessing?"

The traveler let his gaze caress each loving face seated around the table. In the glow of the special candles they seemed to him like precious jewels. This time with them was the most special communion of the week. He would savor every moment. With a tender smile, he bowed his head and began to pray.

"Heavenly Father, My Father . . ."

1

Why Celebrate the Sabbath?

What is a celebration?

Have you ever planned a celebration? Maybe your boss was retiring, or maybe your child was having a birthday, or maybe your parents were passing a milestone anniversary. The scenario probably went something like this: Days, weeks, or, hopefully, a month or so in advance, you began to plan the celebration to the last detail. You thought about the food you would serve, the decorations you would have, the people you would invite, the kind of entertainment you would have and the socializing you would do.

As the event approached, the excitement heightened. You arranged last-minute details. You put the finishing touches on the decorations. You made sure everything was in readiness for the special event. Nothing was left to chance. Just before the celebration was scheduled to begin, you took a shower, put on your best clothes, and made every attempt to look as festive as you felt.

Because of your meticulous planning, the celebration was a suc-

cess. Photos captured the wonderful time everyone had. The hon-
oree thinks back on the event as a special time, and you have fond
remembrances that continue to bring a warm glow to your being
every time you reflect on that special time.

Now let's think about last Sabbath.

Since I can't begin to imagine what yours was like, you can remi-
nisce along with me. Friday—preparation day—I managed to prepare both the Friday evening meal and Sabbath afternoon lunch.
The house was reasonably clean. The children had baths.

Usually, we have a time of welcoming in the Sabbath when I get
out my guitar and we sing songs. After that we read from a devotional book about God's creatures and have prayer. This particular
Friday night, Rachel's teeth were bothering her, and by the time we
got her to stop screaming and go to sleep, it was time to put Josh to
bed as well. We settled for reading some stories from Uncle Arthur,
and then we all went to bed.

Sabbath morning, Rob let me sleep in because Rachel had gotten
me up numerous times during the night to nurse. By the time I got
up, it was time to nurse Rachel again and put her down for her nap.
Rob and Josh went to church ahead of us. I had breakfast, read from
a Christian parenting magazine, and got ready for church while Rachel
slept. Then we joined "the boys" at church, where we were able to
listen to about five minutes of the sermon between quieting the children and keeping them occupied.

After church we came home, had lunch, and all took naps. We
did manage to have our worship to close Sabbath, which follows the
same pattern as the one which opens Sabbath. Shortly after that, the
sun sank behind the mountains, and the Sabbath was over.

Now, not every Sabbath is such a poor example as that one was, but in my opinion you could pick any one of a hundred, and it would be but a moon-cast shadow of what it could be. And it's not God we are shorting—it is ourselves.

"**Blessed** is the man who does this, the man who holds it fast, who keeps the Sabbath without desecrating it, and keeps his hand from doing any evil" (Isaiah 56:2, emphasis mine).

The Sabbath is a blessing. Crafted especially for us. What is a blessing, you might very well ask, because in this day and age it would be highly unlikely (though extremely praiseworthy) if the people in your life actually recited blessings over you. The blessing has somewhat lost its meaning, becoming merely an interchangeable term for grace before meals. Here's one dictionary's definition:

> *Blessing: 1. a. The act of one who blesses. b. The prescribed words of ceremony for such an act. 2. An expression or utterance of good wishes. 3. A special favor granted by God. 4. Something promoting or contributing to happiness, well-being, or prosperity. 5. Approbation; approval. 6. A short prayer before or after a meal.*
> —The American Heritage Dictionary

"**Prescribed words of ceremony.**" This says to me that a blessing isn't an afterthought or simple well-wishing. We Christians often say "God bless you" with as much sincerity as "gesundheit!" A blessing, in comparison, uses special "prescribed" language. The very act of blessing is a ceremony.

"To recite a blessing is a very serious thing," Rabbi Goldberg told me. "If you were to recite a blessing for something you don't need—

for example, if you were to recite a blessing for a piece of bread and then you didn't eat it, that is a sin. Because every blessing contains the name of God. If you recite a blessing for something you do not need—like for the bread you did not eat—it is taking God's name in vain. So a blessing is not said lightly."

"**Special favor granted by God.**" Little children sing "Sabbath is a special day, special day, special day. Sabbath is a special day. I love every Sabbath." For six days a week, we have the opportunity to walk and talk and work with Jesus, but on Sabbath, the day He set apart, He meets with us just to be with us, to refresh us, to celebrate with us. The thousands of things that haunt us, the multiple forms of media that clamor for our attention, the need to do, to find, and to see is stilled for twenty-four hours as the God of the universe stoops low to meet with us for a weekly spiritual date. I think that's pretty special favor.

"**Promoting or contributing to happiness, well-being, or prosperity.**" Inherent in the Sabbath is happiness, well-being, and prosperity:

> "If you keep your feet from breaking the Sabbath and from doing as you please on my holy day, if you call the Sabbath a delight and the Lord's holy day honorable, and if you honor it by not going your own way and not doing as you please or speaking idle words, then you will find your joy in the Lord, and I will cause you to ride on the heights of the land and to feast on the inheritance of your father Jacob." The mouth of the Lord has spoken (Isaiah 58:13, 14).

So the Sabbath is a blessing. Just what does God's blessing bring to us?

He will love you and bless you and [1] increase your numbers. He will bless the fruit of your womb, the crops of your land—[2] your grain, new wine and oil—the calves of your herds and the lambs of your flocks in the land that he swore to your forefathers to give you. You will be blessed more than any other people; none of your men or women will be childless, nor any of your livestock without young. The Lord will [3] keep you free from every disease. He will not inflict on you the horrible diseases you knew in Egypt, but he will inflict them on all who hate you (Deuteronomy 7:13-15).

Notice the three blessings in the above scripture:
1. God will bless your children.
2. God will bless you in your employment.
3. God will give you health and keep you free from disease.

In the Old Testament the Sabbath functioned as a symbol of redemption because it contains God's original promise of the blessing and sanctification of mankind. The scripture says: "God blessed the seventh day and hallowed it" (Gen. 2:3). God's blessing is not just a good wish, like our human blessings, but a concrete assurance of happy and abundant life. The Psalmist declares: "The Lord has commanded the blessing, life for evermore" (Ps. 133:3). Being the symbol of God's gift of abundant life, when Eden was lost, the Sabbath, remained as God's assurance to restore life to his creatures.[1]

Keeping the Sabbath results in many blessings for us. But there

---

1. Samuele Bacchiocchi, Divine Rest for Human Restlessness: The Good News of the Sabbath, (Berrien Springs, Mich.: Biblical Perspectives).

is a big difference between keeping and celebrating the Sabbath. We'll discuss the difference more later on.

Why should we celebrate the Sabbath?

Oh great, you may think, just what we need, another thing to do on Sabbath. Why, we've barely got enough time to study for our Sabbath School lesson or prepare for special music or get our lesson plans together as it is, and here she is saying we should be putting on an entire celebration every Friday night. Just what we need.

Isn't it?

It's very simple to get into a comfortable pattern of observing Sabbath. Friday night comes, and the easy chair looks mighty inviting after a hard week at work. And what's an extra hour or so of sleep on Sabbath morning? You earned it by working so hard all week. Besides, the Sabbath is for resting, isn't it? What's the big deal? So you miss the opening exercises of Sabbath School. You're still there for the entire lesson, aren't you?

And so what if you nod off once or twice during the sermon. I mean, look at Brother So-And-So. Why, he nearly snores every week. And what's the harm of going with nonchurch friends to the beach? You could just as easily go with a group from church if one wanted to go. Besides, a church group would spend the whole time talking about secular subjects anyway. What's the difference? And it's not like you go every week. Some weeks you take walks in the woods or go sing at the nursing home. You pay your dues.

As sundown approaches on Sabbath evening, you can hear an announcer counting down . . . "10, 9, 8, 7, 6, 5, 4, 3, 2, 1! We have lift-off!" And you shoot out of the bonds of tiresome inactivity to do something fun before the whole weekend is shot.

Why Celebrate the Sabbath?

What would you do, how would you feel, if at the stroke of sundown this Friday night you were suddenly transported into the midst of a group of people who were celebrating—I mean really celebrating—the beginning of the Sabbath. What would your reaction be? Would you want to run? Or would your spirit rejoice that it had found kindred souls on the earth?

Don't think of celebration as "just another thing you've got to do." You wouldn't think of your child's birthday party or your wedding ceremony that way. Celebration is more an attitude and less a bunch of activities to do. After all, you can get married anywhere you choose, with or without elaborate decorations, among friends or with just a few witnesses. It's the *spirit* of the participants that marks it as a celebration. They are full of joy and exuberance, love and happiness.

Celebration of our special time together with God recharges us and fills us with energy to meet the demands of the coming week—much like a short break from our work. You know how it happens—you're hard at work but so tired that your productivity starts to slide backward. So you get up from your desk, maybe chat with a neighbor down the hall, get a drink of water from the cooler, and stretch your legs. When you return to your work, you catch your second wind and go right on.

The Sabbath is the jewel of the week. Spending the set-apart hours of the Sabbath with God gives us our second wind. With it we can push through the upcoming week with renewed vigor.

Why aren't we celebrating?

Have you ever been an unexpected guest? As your host hurried and scurried, alternating plans to accommodate you, did you feel somewhat embarrassed? Maybe, you thought, you should have politely declined or taken a rain check. What if there isn't enough food? They weren't planning on you, after all. As the minutes tick by and your host keeps up a steady stream of conversation to divert you from noticing all the compensatory activities, you squirm uncomfortably and begin to feel really guilty for causing all this extra work.

The only scenario I could imagine that would be worse was if the host had invited you and then forgotten you were coming. Or if the family had been too busy during the week and hadn't had time to make the necessary arrangements for your visit. Can you imagine the horrible embarrassment of that? While they are racing around trying to fit you into their plans, all you can think of is squeezing through a crack in the woodwork and disappearing.

But what if you are the host and Jesus is the unexpected guest? How do you think it makes Him feel when He arrives each Friday evening to find us as one of the otherwise occupied characters in the prologue? It isn't as if He springs the time on us like a pop quiz. "*OK, you get a few extra points for planning to have worship, but we've got to deduct some points for not getting everything done by the time the sun set.*" Hardly. The time is set up ahead of time, every week. We have no excuse for forgetting.

Not planning, on the other hand . . . we have many excuses for not planning. Those are a dime a dozen. "I was too busy. My kids were sick. I didn't feel well. I had company this week."

Felicia loved her daughter Ana very much. When Ana graduated from college, she expected her mother to throw her a big party to celebrate. Felicia had promised, and the whole family, as well as many friends, had been eagerly awaiting the party. Ana's anticipation turned to bitter disappointment when she returned to her mother's house and found that her mother had been too busy to plan the party; she didn't feel well, and she'd had company the week before and didn't have time.

Doesn't sound so plausible in the face of reality, does it? Personally, I would wonder just how much Felicia really loved Ana. And I wonder just how much we love God. I am not excluding myself. There are weeks I "endure" the Sabbath hours. There are weeks I'd just like to skip the whole thing or withdraw from life.

One of the biggest factors, I feel, in whether or not we are able to enter into the Sabbath with a spirit of celebration is how we spent the hours of the week preceding it. I know if I haven't taken time to spend with Jesus during the week, the last thing I want to do is celebrate the Sabbath with Him. However, if I have been working on my relationship with Him during the week, I can't wait for the Sabbath. We'll talk more about that in a later chapter.

But is all this really necessary? you might ask. The answer is that it all depends.

Are you content with crumbs?

We are the children of a King, yet we scrabble for scraps beneath His table instead of pulling up a chair and eating with the family. Unlimited resources, that's what we have with Jesus. We are the children of a King, tremendously rich. We do not need to skulk on the edges of Sabbath joy when we have inherited all of it.

Won't you claim your inheritance with me?

CHAPTER

2

What Are We Celebrating?

Maybe, you're thinking, she's got something here. Maybe the Sabbath is a celebration. But a celebration of what? Just what are we supposed to be celebrating? After all, a celebration usually stems from something, not the other way around. People don't decide to have a wedding party before they decide to get married. Students don't have graduation parties before they graduate. What exactly are we celebrating?

The Christian who loves the Savior experiences the Sabbath as a day of joyful celebration: a day to *celebrate the Good News of God's marvelous accomplishments both in the world and in his/her personal life*. It is a human desire to wish to celebrate and share with others the good news of unusual achievements. Players and fans celebrate the winning of a game. A father celebrates the birth of his newborn. Students celebrate their graduation. A couple celebrates with their friends their engagement or wedding. A Christian *celebrates on the Sabbath the Good News of what God has done, of what He is doing and of what He will do for His people*[2] (emphasis mine).

Stop a minute and read the above quote again. Notice particularly the emphasized parts. What is it we're celebrating?

God's marvelous accomplishments both in the world and in our personal lives.

- The Good News of what God has done.
- The Good News of what He is doing.
- The Good News of what He will do for His people.

God's marvelous accomplishments

Let's take this a step further. What *is* God doing? What are His marvelous accomplishments in the world and in our personal lives? I can't answer that question for you. Take some time to think about it and then write them down.

Some of God's marvelous accomplishments in the world:

_____

_____

_____

_____

_____

_____

2. Samuele Bacchiocchi, "Divine Rest for Human Restlessness: The Good News of the Sabbath" (Berrien Springs, Mich.: Biblical Perspectives).

Some of God's marvelous accomplishments in my life:

_____

_____

_____

It is impossible for us, as Christians, to miss seeing God's marvelous accomplishments both in the world and in our personal lives because we should be looking for them. Certainly every day brings news of fresh disasters, crime, and sadness; but it also brings news of God working through His children to help alleviate some of the world's despair.

Each of the things you have written above should be a cause of rejoicing, both today and on Sabbath. If it was hard for you to find any of God's accomplishments, marvelous or otherwise, in the world or your life, you may not be looking in the right place. Seeing with eyes of praise takes some practice. David tells us:

> Praise the Lord. Praise God in his sanctuary; praise him in his mighty heavens. Praise him for his acts of power; praise him for his surpassing greatness. Praise him with the sounding of the trumpet, praise him with the harp and lyre, praise him with tambourine and dancing, praise him with the strings and flute, praise him with the clash of cymbals, praise him with resounding cymbals. Let everything that has breath praise the Lord. Praise the Lord (Psalm 150).

The Good News of what God has done

The biggest reason I don't read the newspaper or watch the news on television is that it's too depressing. The news is a punch list of natural and man-made disasters. It is so rare anything good is ever reported that if you compiled all of those stories, you would be lucky to fill an entire broadcast over the course of a year. My life can be depressing enough. I don't need anything more depressing. I need good news.

The first good news that is proclaimed by the Sabbath is that in the beginning God created our world and everything in it in a perfect and complete way. God's creation lacked nothing. God called it "very good," perfectly satisfying. The NIV text note says:

> God rested on the seventh day, not because he was weary, but because nothing formless or empty remained. His created work was completed—and it was totally effective, absolutely perfect, "very good" (1:31). It did not have to be repeated, repaired or revised, and the Creator rested to commemorate it.[3]

The Hebrew verb "shâbath" means that God stopped or ceased creating. His dramatic action, ceasing creation, testified to the fact that He regarded His creation as perfect. What a fantastic message for us! Not only did God create us—we are not evolved from hairy armpit scratchers—but He created us perfect, lacking nothing.

Our roots go back to God. We didn't get here by chance, flukes of nature, climbing up from primordial soup to become human beings. God *created* us. We are His personal creations. We are rooted in God from creation and into eternity. No matter how futile life here seems, how fragile and fraught with tragedy, our life has great value, meaning, and hope because it comes from

---

3. New International Version Study Bible (Grand Rapids, Mich.: Zondervan Publishing House, 1985).

God and moves toward Him in a final glorious destiny.

Is that Good News or what?

The Good News of what He is doing

The second message that the Sabbath proclaims is that God has redeemed us completely through Jesus. Have you ever heard people (maybe you have been one of them) who constantly ask, "Am I really saved? How do I know I'm really saved? How can I be *sure?*" We want to be sure of salvation. Who could blame us?

One positively vital function of the Sabbath has been to assure us that we have been redeemed by God. We are His people. In the Old Testament, the Sabbath kept alive the hope of salvation to come and pointed to the Deliverer.

Rabbi Heschel captures vividly the Old Testament Messianic typology of the Sabbath when he writes:

> Zion is in ruins, Jerusalem lies in the dust. All week there is only hope of redemption. But when the Sabbath is entering the world, man is touched by a moment of actual redemption; as if for a moment the spirit of the Messiah moved over the face of the earth.[4]

In the New Testament, the Sabbath proclaims that salvation is here and invites us to experience the reality of redemption. In Luke, when Jesus inaugurated His public ministry, it was on a Sabbath day. He read a Sabbatical passage in Isaiah:

---

4. Samuele Bacchiocchi, "Divine Rest for Human Restlessness: The Good News of the Sabbath" (Berrien Springs, Mich.: Biblical Perspectives).

The Spirit of the Sovereign Lord is on me, because the Lord has anointed me to preach good news to the poor. He has sent me to bind up the brokenhearted, to proclaim freedom for the captives and release from darkness for the prisoners, to proclaim the year of the Lord's favor (Isaiah 61:1, 2).

After reading this passage, He rolled the scroll back up, handed it to the attendant, and proclaimed, " 'Today this scripture is fulfilled in your hearing' " (Luke 4:21).

Jesus made it a point to act against the prevailing tradition by healing on the Sabbath. He did it deliberately, not in defiance of the very real obligations of the Sabbath commandment but in order to restore the day to what God intended it to be. The people He healed were chronically ill, in bondage to Satan physically and spiritually. By offering them physical and spiritual liberation, He made the Sabbath a time to celebrate and experience the blessings of His redemptive ministry. His message to us, then and now, is that we are a saved, free people! That is certainly something worth celebrating.

The Good News of what He will do for His people

The third Sabbath message is that God is working to restore the world to its original state of perfection. Jesus told the Jews this after healing the man at the pool of Bethesda.

So, because Jesus was doing these things on the Sabbath, the Jews persecuted him. Jesus said to them, "My Father is always at his work to this very day, and I, too, am working" (John 5:16, 17).

What Are We Celebrating?

Although God rested from His act of Creation on the Sabbath, His work on our behalf has not ceased. The Sabbath reminds us each week that God continues to work on our behalf. It also acts as an invitation to participate with God in accomplishing His restoration in our lives and the lives of others. In John, Jesus invites us to take part in the divine restoration process: " 'As long as it is day, we must do the work of him who sent me. Night is coming, when no one can work' " (John 9:4).

Not only are we reminded each Sabbath that God is working tirelessly to bring us home again, but He invites us to reach out and tell others the Good News! Death, devastation, tragedy, disaster, famine, war, murder, theft, and whatever Satan can throw at us can't steal our peace, can't steal our hope. Every week, through the Sabbath, God reassures us that Satan has lost. We don't need to fear him.

"There remains, then, a Sabbath-rest for the people of God" (Hebrews 4:9).

Through the chaos of everyday life the Sabbath shines like a beacon, pointing straight to God, reminding us that He is in control. He was in control at Creation, He was in control at the Cross, and our future is in His hands. We have nothing to fear. No matter what happens here on earth, God is in control of this world, working out His plan and purpose.

We have three reasons to celebrate on the Sabbath: (1) God has created us perfectly, (2) He has redeemed us completely, and (3) He will restore us ultimately. Each week He invites us to joyfully celebrate these things with Him.

Creation. Redemption. Restoration. We've got an awful lot to celebrate.

CHAPTER

3

Preparing to Celebrate

It's Who you know

With the week bearing down like an out-of-control freight train, it isn't hard to forget all about Sabbath until five minutes before sundown. Life is vicious. It takes no prisoners. There is always something to do or someone to talk to. It can seem like it never ends, just cycling continuously from morning until evening, with hardly time to squeeze in simple pleasures like breathing, eating, and sleeping.

There are more things competing for our attention today than ever. Whereas a little over a century ago the most complicated communication device was the telephone, today the ways information assaults us are practically endless. From junk mail to spam, just wading though it can be a full-time job. Before you know it, twenty-four are missing and then forty-eight, and before you know it, Sabbath again.

At the very beginning of the fourth commandment the Lord said, "Remember." He knew that amid the multitude of cares and perplexities man would be tempted to excuse himself from meeting the full requirement of the law, or would forget its sacred importance. Therefore He said, "Remember the Sabbath day, to keep it holy." Exodus 20:8.

All through the week we are to have the Sabbath in mind and be making preparation to keep it according to the commandment. We are not merely to observe the Sabbath as a legal matter. We are to understand its spiritual bearing upon all the transactions of life. All who regard the Sabbath as a sign between them and God, showing that He is the God who sanctifies them, will represent the principles of His government. They will bring into daily practice the laws of His kingdom. Daily it will be their prayer that the sanctification of the Sabbath may rest upon them. Every day they will have the companionship of Christ and will exemplify the perfection of His character. Every day their light will shine forth to others in good works.[5]

The key being, I think, the remembering. All through the week. Not just on Thursday night. Not just on Friday morning. Not five minutes before sundown. But all week long. Because the Sabbath isn't just a twenty-four hour time slot. It's the whipped cream on the sundae, the crème fraiche on the pie. It isn't separate from the week. It completes the week.

And that's where daily spending time with Jesus comes in. I hesitate to say we need to have a "relationship" with Him, because that's

---

5. Ellen G. White, *Testimonies for the Church*, (Nampa, Idaho: Pacific Press® Publishing Association, 1948), 6:353, 354.

become such an often repeated prescription that it doesn't mean much anymore. We have, to some extent, "relationships" with lots of people: co-workers, family, friends, the guy at the newspaper stand, the dentist, our vet. Just having a relationship doesn't guarantee that you will be close to someone.

Unfortunately, in our world of high speed and high tech, most of us have lost our ability to have a really close relationship with someone. We're lucky if we can pull it off with just one person, and that is usually with our spouse. The fact that it is just as often not with our spouse is the greatest contributing factor in the rising divorce rate.

Relationships are hungry animals. You can't feed them sporadically with tidbits when you have time or feel in the mood and expect them to grow. They won't. And a relationship with Jesus isn't any different than a relationship with anyone else you know. Just because He's God doesn't mean He'll take up the lion's share of the work involved in maintaining a relationship because you're too busy doing something else.

As in every other relationship in life, I've got to put in quality if I expect to get quality. Quantity doesn't hurt either. A relationship with Jesus can fizzle and die just like any other relationship that's neglected and taken advantage of. The only difference is that the end of this relationship has eternal consequences.

When I get up in the morning, it's not enough to check off "Offered my will to God" or "Dedicated myself and my family to God today," as though in the checking off it was all accomplished. It's not.

God wants me so surrendered to Him that when I wake up, He's the first and most all-consuming thought I have. He wants to be so central in my life that I wouldn't dream of beginning my day without Him any more than I would think of hiking to the North Pole in shorts and a T-shirt. He doesn't want me to "remember" to consecrate my day to Him each morning. He wants to be such a priority that I would be bereft if something prevented our coming together.

He wants me to surround myself with Him. He wants to be the vortex of my life, with everything else just swirling around the edges. Eventually He's going to draw in everything in my life, every part of it, until it's all His. And the bad stuff will go right down the drain.

That's the kind of "relationship" God wants to have with us. Is that the kind of relationship you want to have with God? Take a minute and think about that because a pat answer won't do here. We tend to look with high scorn and deep pity on Israel of old because she just never could quite get it right. Always chasing after what she wasn't supposed to have, she thought it was possible to worship God right along with other deities in a syncretistic way.

> Elijah went before the people and said, "How long will you waver between two opinions? If the Lord is God, follow him; but if Baal is God, follow him." *But, the people said nothing* (1 Kings 18:21, emphasis mine).

It's easy to think we're right on God's heels, stuck tighter to Him than a blister. We're Seventh-day Adventists, after all, not old-time Israelites. And that usually lasts until someone says, "Oh, you're a Seventh-day Adventist. You guys don't . . ."

Well. Well, some of us do and some of us don't. So, what is it? A health message or a nice thought? A lifestyle practice or a hopeless, but pretty, ideal? Biblical command or a rule with a lot of give?

Let's make up our minds. Are we following God or Baal? The

time has gone by to say nothing. It's time to make a decision one way or another. And the way we make that decision is by our choices. There is a judgment coming soon, and it's not going to be based on what we claimed to believe. It's going to be based on what we did.

And the most important of the things that we do is our relationship with Jesus. Because what we do with that, whether we work to make it stronger or give up and let it die, is going to affect the rest of what we do. What we do and who we are stem from our roots in Jesus. All our actions flow from that. Not the other way around. We can't work ourselves into a relationship with Jesus by working for Him. We must start with Him and take it from there.

Preparation is the key

Another element that tops the list of being ready for Sabbath celebration is cleaning. The best book I have ever read on the subject is Oh No, *It's Sabbath Again, and I'm Not Ready!*, by Yara Cerna Young (Pacific Press®). The book's claim to be "a homemaker's guide to making Friday the easiest day of the week" is not lightly made.

Unfortunately, this book is no longer in print. I spoke with Yara Young, who continues to travel around the country giving seminars on home organization and Sabbath preparation. She informed me that she still has a set of four tapes that provides much of the information contained in the book, and if enough people contact her, she will reproduce them.[6]

Certainly, having an orderly house goes a long way to Sabbath peace and being able to celebrate without reservation. Running

---

6. To contact Yara Young about the possibility of getting a tape set, write: Yara Young, 12717 Oakmont Drive, Kansas City, MO 64145.

around at the last minute trying to squeeze in a few final chores is probably the most common reason for infringing on the Sabbath hours. We cringe and scurry around, all the time waiting for a booming voice to condemn us and a lightning bolt to strike us. But it isn't that God is going to punish us. We cheat ourselves.

So how can we protect the fringes of the Sabbath? By being prepared. And being prepared is not something that just happens. You have to work at it.

> The most important home-organization idea in this book can be stated simply in ten words: The night before is the key to the next day. This idea will make the difference between success and failure. All that you will read in the rest of this book will be effective largely to the degree that you heed this concept religiously.
>
> What does this mean—The night before is the key to the next day? It means that if we tidy up the house in the evening before going to bed, then maintaining the home will be simple. We will be "ahead of the game." If we fail to tidy up the house in the evening before going to bed, then we will have a more difficult time. We will be "behind the eight ball."[7]

While each day has a specific task and Young outlines ways to keep household clutter (toys, clothes, laundry) in hand, the most important thing, she claims, is tidying up the house in the evening. She begins before her children are in bed for the night. They pick up their toys while she straightens out anything that has been used dur-

---

7. Yara Cerna Young, *Oh No, It's Sabbath Again and I'm Not Ready!* (Nampa, Idaho: Pacific Press® Publishing Association, 1992), 27.

ing the day. After the children are in bed, she sets the table for breakfast(!), does the supper dishes, and ties up loose ends: folding laundry, putting beans or whole grains in the Crock-Pot for one of tomorrow's meals.

Another cornerstone of Young's book is that preparing for Sabbath begins on Monday. The way her schedule works, Friday is the easiest cleaning day of the week. That leaves time for other things, like cooking.

> While preparation for the Sabbath is to be made all through the week, Friday is to be the special preparation day. Through Moses the Lord said to the children of Israel: "Tomorrow is the rest of the holy Sabbath unto the Lord: bake that which ye will bake today, and seethe that ye will seethe; and that which remaineth over lay up for you to be kept until the morning." "And the people went about, and gathered it [the manna], and ground it in mills, or beat it in a mortar, and baked it in pans, and made cakes of it." Exodus 16:23; Numbers 11:8. There was something to be done in preparing the heaven-sent bread for the children of Israel. The Lord told them that this work must be done on Friday, the preparation day. This was a test to them. God desired to see whether or not they would keep the Sabbath holy.[8]

Meals are certainly a concern, but with preparation and planning it is possible to have everything ready for Sabbath. The Jewish housewife certainly had it harder than we do, and she always managed.

---

8. *Testimonies for the Church*, 6:354, 355.

Work is prohibited on the Sabbath. This means that the lighting of fires is forbidden, as is cooking in most senses of the word. It would, of course, be possible to satisfy these basic conditions by eating cold leftovers, so long as they were normally kosher. But the Sabbath is not meant as a day of suffering, so special efforts are made to serve hot food whose preparation does not involve cooking or lighting fires.

The Sabbath begins at sundown on Friday, which means that the Friday evening meal is not particularly difficult to bring off in accordance with the [S]abbath rules. The Jewish wife gets her meal underway in the afternoon and plans it so that her work for it ends before dark. The problem meal is Saturday lunch. The solution is a filling one-pot dish whose prep work can be completed before sundown on Friday. From there on, for the ensuing 16 to 20 hours, the covered dish cooks slowly, in an oven or on top of the stove over an asbestos pad or other heat diminishing device (the Yiddish name for this is blech, for tin or sheet metal).[9]

Now, our Sabbath food preparation rules are not as stringent as the Jewish housewife's. It's probably been a long time since any of us has used a blech. I don't know anyone who is concerned with heating food on the Sabbath. We are more likely to debate whether or not to do the dishes or leave them until after Sabbath.

The Friday evening meal can be anything you desire but should be fairly simple. Soup or spaghetti is nice, but anything your family likes is great. At our house, I generally make bread, particularly in

---

9. Raymond Sokolov, *The Jewish American Kitchen*, (Wings Books, 1993), 22, 23.

the winter, and we are apt to have soup and challah or focaccia bread.

Although the food doesn't need to be fancy, this is not the time for paper plates. Consider having a formal meal. Leave the paper plates and plastic dishware for weekdays. On the Sabbath, dress the table with your best. You're expecting an important Guest.

The Sabbath meal is easy to make ahead of time if you prepare a casserole or other one-dish entree. This only needs to be reheated or cooked, whichever is quicker. Ingredients for a salad can be washed and chopped the day before and stored in separate bags in the fridge to be combined just before Sabbath lunch. Things like garlic bread can also be done ahead of time, sliced, buttered, sprinkled with garlic, and then wrapped and placed in the fridge. Juice, if you are having it, can be mixed up ahead of time.

If possible, plan your cooking and food preparations for Friday. Your cleaning will be done, and you can spend the rest of your day largely with your children, preparing them for Sabbath. Then when sundown comes, you will be ready to celebrate and not worn down with cleaning.

Preparing children for the Sabbath

Rachel, who is thirteen months right now, loves to have worship. All I have to do is tell her it is time for worship, and before I can take down the felt board, she is clapping her hands and smiling. Joshua's favorite part is learning his memory verse. When he was younger, he chose stickers and was allowed to put one up every time he said his memory verse. I have charts full of stickers that he enjoys looking at even today.

We have worship every day. It basically consists of the lesson in felts, the memory verse, singing, and prayer. The length is guided by the smallest member, but she usually pushes the limits of singing by demanding more songs. The children have rhythm instruments they play while we sing, and I try to add to their collection periodically.

Besides daily worship, we have prayer times with the children before naps and going to bed for the night. If we are all together in the morning, which happens more when the kids sleep through the night, my husband will gather us all around and say prayer before he goes to work (or I go to work, depending on the schedule). As well as these things, I try to keep an open mind to teachable moments and make the best of them.

Joshua, like most four-year-olds, has an active, inquisitive mind. Almost anything can be an object lesson if you seize it. I used to feel silly bringing Jesus into every conversation, the same way I used to feel silly reading Bible storybooks to my pregnant belly.

"Mom, why is the sky blue?"

"Because that's the color Jesus made it."

"Mom, why do some animals eat other animals?"

"The animals didn't always eat each other, honey. When Jesus made them in the Garden of Eden, there was no death, so none of the animals killed the other ones. But because of sin, now some of the animals eat other animals. It's sad, I know, but if they didn't, then there would be too many of some animals and they would starve to death because there wasn't enough food for them. In heaven, the animals won't eat each other. Isn't that great?"

Granted, he may not always understand my explanations, but I hope he always gets one message: Everything somehow ties in to Jesus and what He made for us, gave us, is doing for us, will do for us, etc. It always goes back to Jesus. And the more I answer questions based on this criteria, the easier it gets and the more natural it seems.

In all that pertains to the success of God's work, the very first victories are to be won in the home life. Here the preparation for the Sabbath must begin. Throughout the week let parents remember that their home is to be a school in which their children shall be prepared for the courts above. Let their words be right words. No words which their children should not hear are to escape their lips. Let the spirit be kept free from irritation. Parents, during the week live as in the sight of a holy God, who has given you children to train for Him. Train for Him the little church in your home, that on the Sabbath all may be prepared to worship in the Lord's sanctuary. Each morning and evening present your children to God as His blood-bought heritage. Teach them that it is their highest duty and privilege to love and serve God.[10]

If we go about it right, with God's help, we can raise our children to naturally turn to Him, rely on Him, and converse with Him. But it's got to be natural to us first. And that may be the hardest part. I know I was not brought up to seek God first in everything, although mine was a Christian family. It is hard, therefore, to teach my children that when I have to constantly remind myself first.

However, I know that with God's help I can do it, for myself and for them. It thrills God when I ask Him to help me raise the children He's given me. After all, they are His children first, and He knows perfectly how best to raise them so their hearts will turn toward Him.

We are so pressured by society to do, to have, and to accomplish that even with the best of intentions, our priorities can be rearranged

---

10. *Testimonies for the Church*, 6:354.

without our even being aware of it. If I don't take a constant inventory, I often find myself amazed at how little what I say that is important to me matches what I spend my time and energy on. In an average day, most of my attention is taken up by the things I would consider least important to me. Only when I am constantly on guard can I make choices that will bring my actions in line with my priorities.

It is this same diligence that has to be applied to preparing our children for Sabbath. Unless we are proactive about making Sabbath inviting, they are likely to see it as a day of "don'ts." As we are cleaning or cooking or preparing special things for our Sabbath celebration, we need to include our children. We need to be constantly striving to turn their hearts toward us and toward God and His special day.

Answer their questions and let them get involved. Sing Sabbath or preparation songs. Keep a positive attitude; keep your heart turned towards your child. Children will respond to a negative attitude even quicker than they will respond to a positive one.

A lot of their reaction and response to Sabbath depends on our own attitude about it. If we see Sabbath as a drudgery, then that is how our children will see it. If celebrating the Sabbath is exciting to us, then that excitement will be caught by our children.

Case in point: Have you ever seen a child who was not excited about Christmas?

Put away differences

There is something else that needs to be done before the Sabbath can be truly celebrated.

There is another work that should receive attention on the preparation day. On this day all differences between brethren, whether in the family or in the church, should be put away. Let all bitterness and wrath and malice be expelled from the soul. In a humble spirit, "confess your faults one to another, and pray one for another, that ye may be healed." James 5:16.[11]

I think most of us know what this means. Living as we do, close to the heart of God, we will know when we have sinned against a brother or sister or when they have sinned against us. When that happens we have an obligation.

"If you forgive men when they sin against you, your heavenly Father will also forgive you. But if you do not forgive men their sins, your Father will not forgive your sins" (Matthew 6:14, 15).

We must freely forgive one another. And while most of us know the process that entails, which Jesus outlined in Matthew 18:15-17, I think we often confuse forgiveness with trust. My friend Jennifer Jill Schwirzer, singer/songwriter, says it this way in an article she wrote about abusers, but I feel it speaks to everyone who has been wronged.

It is plain that forgiving others and being forgiven by God come in the same package. You can't have one without the other. Yes, God calls you to forgive those who have violated you. But—and this is important—He does not call you to trust them. There is a difference between forgiveness and trust. Forgiveness is unconditionally given, trust is not. Especially

---

11. Ibid., 356.

when trust has been violated, it is re-established on condition.

I am boldly claiming your right, as a Christian, to distrust those who have broken trust. You forgive them because Jesus forgave everyone, including His murderers (see Luke 23:34). But Jesus did not trust His tormentors. He spent most of His ministry avoiding them, especially when they tried to hurt Him.[12]

In confusing forgiveness with trust, I think many of us make it harder to offer the forgiveness. We have this picture in our heads of Christian doormats who forgive "seventy times seven" because that's what Jesus asks us to do. And we should. But that doesn't mean that we are to allow people to tread all over us, wiping the scum off their boots and generally ill-abusing us.

This year we have had a very painful time with a member of our family who is participating in blatant sins and destructive behavior, which ripped our extended family apart. This person stole from us, undermined our business, and treated us with deceit. For a long time, I did not think I could forgive this person. If I forgave, it would mean that I had to treat the person just like before, withholding no privilege despite the fact that they had no remorse for what they had done and continued to do. Right?

No.

Forgiving them was easier once I separated forgiveness from trust. I could forgive. Jesus forgave me; how could I not? But trust? This person is in a position to influence my children, continues to sin openly, and feels they have God's blessing while do-

---

12. Jennifer Jill Schwirzer, "Can God Save an Abuser?" Michael Ministries News, November 1997.

ing so. This person considers it their personal duty in life to undermine my husband's and my teaching as Christian parents. No, I could not trust them.

Trust is a touchy thing. You first extend it, like love, knowing full well that it might be betrayed. And sometimes it is. After that it has to be built up slowly. It isn't something that just springs back to its natural position. Sometimes it's possible to regain trust in a short time, but often it takes much time to rebuild what was so carelessly destroyed. It may be impossible. In that case, the person who destroyed it has to accept the fact that those who have been hurt may never completely trust again, and the victim may choose not to reestablish the relationship. That is his/her right.

Odds and ends

While those points cover the bulk of preparing to celebrate the Sabbath, there are various odds and ends you will want to attend to before your celebration. There is a saying that goes, "A place for everything and everything in its place." Being a compulsive organizer, I like that saying a great deal. Its importance in celebrating is that if you must create a celebration from scratch each week, you are not likely to continue the practice.

Once you have decided on a method of celebrating, you will want to keep the tools necessary for that celebration (i.e., candles, matches, special dishes, tablecloth, devotional books, instruments, tapes, CDs) together in a separate place. This way, they are not used for something during the week, leaving you to hunt for them at the last minute.

Another area that requires some preparation is conversation. That's right: simple talking. Before the Sabbath hours, think about things you have learned or studied during the week, and then be prepared to share and discuss them. Take the initiative and change the topic of conversation if you must. There are few things that destroy Sabbath peace and shatter the holy hours like worldly topics of conversation.

Like an itch when your hands are occupied, miscellaneous secular things always occur to us just as the sun divebombs the horizon. One way to deal with things that come to you and must be shared is to write them down on a notepad so that after the Sabbath you will remember to discuss or relate them. Eventually, when Satan can't distract you with them anymore, you will find that it happens less and less.

As much as possible, put away things that would remind you of the world. Drape items like the TV, sewing machine, or computer with a cloth. You can use freshly laundered old sheets, or, if you are creative, make a special covering.

Put secular papers in a drawer. Return secular books to the book case. If you plan to listen to the radio, make sure it is tuned to a Christian station before Sabbath begins. Set a peaceful mood by lighting candles or playing soft, religious music. Let children play quietly with special toys set aside just for Sabbath.

Preparing for Sabbath takes thought, but, most important, it takes a willing spirit. You can drag yourself through a drudgery of "have-to-get-dones," but you will miss the intended blessing of the Sabbath you are working so hard for. Instead, ask yourself daily, "What can I do today that will help to prepare me and my house for Sabbath this week?" knowing that everything you do will help to make the coming Sabbath a mountaintop experience with your Creator.

Including Extended Family Members and Friends

Extending the invitation

I met her for the first time in the grocery store. She had on a long linen dress and was with a little girl, the daughter of one of her housemates. Her thick brown hair was tied back in a simple ponytail. She wore no rings, makeup, no artifices of any kind. Her face was plain and sweet.

She gave me a shy smile and admired my children, asking about how old the baby was. During the course of our conversation, she mentioned that she lived with The Community (which I had guessed already, based on her appearance). The Community is like our self-supporting institutes. Families live together communally, and children work with their "abbas"* making soap and candles.

---

* fathers

"Oh," I exclaimed. "I love your soap! I stopped in the shop last year to get some, and the man I talked to invited me to come over and celebrate the Sabbath with all of you that Friday night. I had planned on going, but I was pregnant, and the night I was going to go we had a family crisis. Shortly after that, I had the baby, so I never did make it."

"You must come," she said eagerly. "The invitation is still open." She said her name was Tsevyah, which means "gazelle" in Hebrew.

We parted with even friendlier smiles, and I promised I would come sometime. That Friday something was going on, and I didn't make it. The following week, I saw my new friend at the grocery store again. "I didn't make it," I said. The line would become a litany of sorts.

As we stood in the produce aisle, Tsevyah pulled a wrinkled invitation out of the cloth bag hanging around her neck. She handed it to me. "The invitation is still open," she repeated.

That invitation is in the file folder I have for this book. It is just a piece of paper folded in fourths like a homemade card. Above a simple drawing of a family and the word Welcome it reads, "Please join us for a special celebration meal and Israeli dancing every Friday evening at 6:00 PM."

There are a few more simple, folksy drawings and the written testimonies of eight people ranging in age from ten to thirty-four about their experience with The Community. On the back are directions and phone numbers for their residences in Rutland and the soap shop.

It dawned on me, standing there among the fruits and vegetables, listening to Tsevyah talk about Yahshua[13] and what The Community

---

13. Although the name of Jesus is usually rendered "Yehshua" in its Hebrew form, the people at The Community believe this may have originally been done as a slur against His name and prefer to use the spelling "Yahshua."

believes, that this is what I should be doing. In the pack I carried to the grocery store were my checkbook, credit cards, a pen, and a few bucks. I wasn't equipped for witnessing as Tsevyah was. I wasn't even particularly attuned to opportunities for it.

Before we can invite others to share the Sabbath with us, we must first have something to share.

Rob and I were married for eight years before we had our first child, Joshua. In those eight years, we never managed to nail down a Sabbath routine. Welcoming the Sabbath was sporadic at best. Closing Sabbath usually only happened if we were at someone else's house. Then along came Joshua. It's interesting how traditions are formed after the advent of children. We started to do for him what we should have done for ourselves all along.

At first we had to remind ourselves to have it. And then we had to tailor it to Josh. Also, we had to persevere when relatives would drop by unannounced (relatives in these parts rarely call first). It was rough. I can recall many worship times that would dissolve at the intrusion of boisterous relatives.

But we stuck it out, and eventually it became something we looked forward to. We keep our eyes open for worship materials that will interest Josh and also appeal to the various adults who congregate at our house at worship time. Worship has been established. It is an unshakable institution. It goes on now regardless of who is at our house or who stops by at a moment's notice.

Like I said, before we can invite others to share the Sabbath with us, we must first have something to share. I know that seems redundant, but think about it. Is your Sabbath a banquet you can lay before guests and invite them to eat freely? Or is it a measly meal of bread crusts and tap water? That isn't to say that we must have an elaborate Sabbath program before we can feel free to invite others to celebrate with us any more than we must have an eight-course meal before we can invite people to dinner. But, we must have something to share.

When you work through the material in chapters 6 and 7, you will get some ideas of how you would like to celebrate the Sabbath. If these are new to you, become comfortable with them before you attempt to invite others to join you. Timidity will put a damper on your ability to become comfortable with the newness of your Sabbath celebrations and could result in a less than pleasant experience.

Once you are ready to invite others to celebrate the Sabbath with you, try out a few of these suggestions:

The invitation. Your invitation to celebrate could be as simple as a verbal "Would you like to come over and open (or close) Sabbath with us?" or something as elaborate as a formal, printed invitation like the one Tsevyah gave me. Both have their place.

A verbal invitation would work well with someone you know—friends, colleagues, acquaintances, family. They aren't likely to need directions to your house. A reminder of the time and a formal invitation would seem stilted in most cases and might, in fact, make them uncomfortable. However, because they won't have something written down for them, be sure to inform them of all the details you might take for granted (Meal? Potluck or provided? Dress? Casual or dressy? If they play an instrument, should they bring it?)

A written invitation has some advantages over a verbal invitation. When Tsevyah handed me her invitation in the grocery store, I was able to take it home and look at it later when I could think about it. It was tangible. Something to look at, read, contemplate. It was not as easy to dismiss as a verbal invitation would have been.

A printed, or written, invitation (they don't have to be as elaborate as a wedding invitation!) can be handed to people you meet, maybe through mutual friends who express interest in the Sabbath. It should include, besides the invitation and a simple explanation of your celebration, your address (a hand-drawn map is a nice touch), your name and phone number, the time you plan to start, and any other details you feel inclined to share.

Making invitations is a great activity for children and a wonderful way to get them involved in inviting people to celebrate the Sabbath with you. If you have a computer, you can design them on any number of printing programs. If you don't have a computer or if you would rather have a more personal touch, let your children draw pictures and hand-letter the information. (Hint: fold a sample invitation first so you can see where everything should go.) A copy shop can print copies for you (front and back), and all you have left is to fold them and pass them out. If your children have designed the cards, they might be more inclined to give them to friends.

The invitees. Anyone you know, or meet, is a potential invitee to your Sabbath celebration. It mostly depends on who you and your family are comfortable inviting. Some families have the gift of hospitality and have no qualms about inviting perfect strangers to their house for any occasion. Other families get tongue-tied just thinking about having people they don't know in their house, and it takes them months to prepare for things like Thanksgiving and Christmas.

Problems arise when one or more members of the family are outgoing and others aren't. Because celebrating the Sabbath is a family affair first and foremost, it is important to take into account the feelings of all family members before making invitations. Discuss this with family members and decide who you might like to invite to your Sabbath celebration. It should be agreed on ahead of time who can be invited so there are no last-minute surprises. You may wish to begin by inviting another family who has children about the same age. You could even take turns, alternating between your two homes to celebrate.

Once your family is comfortable sharing the Sabbath, discuss who you might invite that would stretch your comfort zone. You may wish to invite someone not as well acquainted with the Sabbath at a time when you are celebrating with others who are already accustomed to celebrating the Sabbath. This should help them feel more at ease because the attention won't all be focused on them.

And don't feel pressured to invite people every week unless that is something you really enjoy. Maybe you will only want to invite others to celebrate with you on special occasions or only once a month. How often is your decision, and each member of the family should be comfortable with it.

5

How Other Religions Celebrate the Sabbath

I wanted to see how other religious groups celebrated the Sabbath in comparison to Seventh-day Adventists. I decided to observe The Community and our local Jewish congregation. I knew that both have Friday evening services to welcome the Sabbath.

My purpose was twofold. First, I wanted to see if there was anything I could bring away from their services that would enhance, or help us establish, our own sundown services. Second, I wanted to see how they viewed Sabbath, what it meant to them and how they observed and/or celebrated it.

The Community

The Community began as the Northeast Kingdom Community Church in Island Pond (located in the Northeast Kingdom of Vermont, hence the name). Though they don't now have an official name, they are generally referred to as The Community. They are a

Messianic community who believes that they are a chosen people who have been called to live together as apostles, sharing everything in common. Their businesses include a soap shop, printing shop, and shoe store.

They have houses in Vermont, Massachusetts, Missouri, Manitoba, France, Brazil, and New Zealand. Other communities are planned. Two of their houses and the soap-making shop are located in Rutland, where I live. About the time they moved here, most of the Sunday section of the newspaper was devoted to their history and beliefs. I was acquainted with them because I had patronized their store in Burlington and had always been curious about the sign in the window that listed their hours and stated, "Closed Sabbath beginning at sundown on Friday."

The newspaper article described how the members clean their households thoroughly on Friday. They gather for a special meal after the evening sacrifice. This sacrifice is offered morning and evening. The members gather to offer themselves as a living sacrifice as described in Romans:

> Therefore, I urge you, brothers, in view of God's mercy, to offer your bodies as living sacrifices, holy and pleasing to God—this is your spiritual act of worship (Romans 12:1).

Their sacrifice consists of prayer and recommitment to God, songs and Israeli folk dancing.

The pictures accompanying the article showed happy, smiling faces. I was intrigued. I would have gone anyway, because they seemed to have something we desperately lack . . . happiness about the Sabbath.

A Friday night

One Friday evening I took Joshua and two loaves of bread and decided to go see what The Community was all about. I pulled into the parking lot of the soap shop. The house is right next door, and already people were gathering out on the lawn. Women wore scarves over their hair, loose blouses, and skirts or long dresses. Their clothes were all fashioned from natural fibers. The men wore cotton trousers (no jeans) and loosely styled cotton shirts. Everyone wore sandals. People were greeting each other with hugs. There were a few curious stares as I got Josh out of the car.

Before I could take two steps, a woman who had been walking from the soap shop to the house redirected her steps and approached me with a smile. "Hello," she said. "Are you from around here?"

"Yes," I replied. "I live in Rutland Town, just down the road. Tsevyah invited me."

"Ah!" Understanding filled her eyes. "How did you meet Tsevyah?"

"At the Jam Can," I replied and then had to interrupt myself to explain that was what we called the local discount food store. Tsevyah caught sight of us and came over, greeting me with a hug.

"I made it finally," I laughed.

"I'm glad. We're almost ready to start the minchâh (the Hebrew word for sacrifice). They just blew the shophar (in English, shofar: a trumpet made from a ram's horn; traditionally blown in the synagogue, at Rosh Hashana, the Jewish New Year festival). Come on over."

We followed Tsevyah over to where the other members were gathered. Many greeted us. I was handed a glass of maté, which is made from green tea, honey, and milk. A man began to talk, reading from a small Bible in his hand and elaborating on the text. When he was through, two men playing guitars jumped into a song, and children and a few adults picked up tambourines and bells and tapped along. A ring of dancers, children as well as adults, moved to the center of the gathering and began an Israeli folk dance.

The music was lively and the verses repeated many times. At the end of the song another man began to speak, also consulting his Bible. There was another song and another speaker. During this entire time the children remained quiet and respectful. I did not see evidence of even a single toy, and the children (there were many of them) ranged in age from nursing infants to teenagers.

After the last speaker and dance, the entire congregation moved closer in a circle, and the men raised their arms toward heaven. (The women do not raise their arms. Tsevyah explained to me that the reason is twofold. First, because the men, being the leaders of their household, are approaching God and the women are under their "umbrella." Second, because the women need to keep their hands free to take care of their little ones.) Shouting, men and women began to praise God and thank Him for their blessings.

"Yahshua, thank You for saving us!"

"Master Yahshua, thank You for giving us Your Sabbath!"

"Thank You for giving us food, Abba."

At the close of the prayer, everyone loudly proclaimed "Amen!"

I mistakenly believed that the celebration was all over. A young girl circulated with homemade crackers and cheese, and then everyone began to take seats at the tables that were spread out beneath the canopy of trees. I sat with Tsevyah. She introduced me to a man named Ehud, who was familiar with Adventist beliefs. He spent the dinner hour trying to explain to me how our beliefs differ.

After dinner, the real celebration began. Inside the soap shop, there is a large, open area. The floor is made of smooth wooden boards. The middle of the floor is kept clear except for the dancers. The "band" consisted of violins, a bass, flutes, guitars, recorder, tambourine, and drum grouped together in one corner.

The dancers gathered around and did what is often called a Hebrew circle dance. Sometimes, if there are too many dancers, the children and a few adults form another circle inside the large one. Most of the steps looked simple and yet complicated. I wanted to dance, but none of the steps were repetitive enough for me to catch on until the dance was over. This didn't prevent Tsevyah from insisting that I try one.

The children called it the Washing Machine Dance because one of the steps is shifting from side to side like a washing machine shaking through the spin cycle. Tsevyah said the actual name was Hora Hagadati. None of that mattered as I tried to figure out the steps while nearly running around the circle. Following Tsevyah's feet proved impossible because her long skirt hid them. By the time I began to manage the steps correctly, the song was over.

But, it was exhilarating. Inhaling the strong odor of peppermint, seeing the laughing, smiling faces. The exuberant joy that lighted them up from the inside was like candles in the darkness. They were all like children, completely without guile, single-minded in their purpose, to worship their Master, Yahshua. A man named Shebet walked into the circle and began to talk.

"I am so happy to be here," he said. "All week has been like climbing a tall mountain. Every step was hard. But today, on the Shabbat, it's like reaching the top of the mountain, and we can see for miles. We can see for miles and miles, and the view is beautiful. Here we can rest and spend time with each other and our Master, Yahshua."

He leapt across the circle, stamping his foot to emphasize his words. "We are so blessed. Our Master, Yahshua, has blessed us so much. He has taught us to live in unity, to live together as brothers and sisters. He has blessed us with these wonderful children who are learning to follow Him and love Him. I'm so proud of these children who are learning to follow the Master."

I tried to picture the people in my church there in that place, worshipping God with so little concern for appearances, but I could not. I don't know if that had to do more with inbred Yankee reticence or the old-fashioned Methodist sobriety that our church's worship roots are buried in. I don't suppose, in the end, God cares as much how we worship Him as that we worship Him at all. But these people reminded me of David, leaping and dancing before God. And I envied them for their carefree, spontaneous, natural worship. It was an extension of their lives, not a separate compartment to be entered into.

After about an hour of celebrating, the dancers broke up and abbas and emmas began to collect their children. Some of the littlest ones had fallen asleep on the long wooden tables in the soap shop. My lungs, scrubbed fresh by the heady scent of peppermint from the soap shop, filled with warm night air. Tsevyah invited me to come back for a Saturday night, and I promised that I would.

A Saturday night

I attended a Saturday night in the middle of January. It was held in The Community's other house, which I had never visited. When I arrived, people were dancing and singing. On Saturday night, a special effort was made to include the children, Yonadab explained to me. The dances and songs were simpler (so simple I easily joined two), some of them started by the children.

All of The Community's houses have two things in common. They are big, and they are old. The ones I have seen are all in some state of renovation. The gathering in this house took place in two rooms that opened into each other that were probably the sitting room and dining room. The rooms were packed with the children and adults dancing in a whirl of color. The whole place reverberated with the singing and stamp of many feet.

"Rejoice and be glad, let's dance and let's sing. Lift up voices and praise Him . . . "

"Yahshua's life was significant," a man said. "He made an impact, and we can live the same way." When the singing and dancing was over, we all crowded into the middle of the room to pray.

After the prayer, Shebet carried in a large wine glass full of wine. This is called the Victory cup. Smiling, he said, "This is the fruit of the vine. When we're pressed during the week, what is going to come out of us is the fruit of the Spirit!"

We all held hands, raised in victory, while Shebet raised the goblet and with the help of another man held it up during the prayer. After, members were offered the cup, and if they felt that they had overcome during the week, they took a drink. If they felt that they had not overcome, they refused, determining to strive harder in the coming week to come to obtain victory in their lives with the help of Yahshua.

Nahara and Yonadab explained what the Victory cup means. Matthew says:

> While they were eating, Jesus took bread, gave thanks and broke it, and gave it to his disciples, saying, "Take and eat;

this is my body." Then he took the cup, gave thanks and offered it to them, saying, "Drink from it, all of you. This is my blood of the covenant, which is poured out for many for the forgiveness of sins. I tell you, I will not drink of this fruit of the vine from now on until that day when I drink it anew with you in my Father's kingdom" (Matthew 26:26-29).

So, the cup signifies the victory of Jesus' death and resurrection and His ongoing victory being lived out in their lives. Even the older children partake. Depending on how old they are, their parents might judge whether or not they have had victory in their lives in the past week. The older ones judge their lives themselves.

After the Victory cup, everyone settled down on the floor to hear Basar tell a story about Moshe (Moses) and the flight of the Israelites from Egypt and their journey through the wilderness. The children gathered in the middle, directly in front of Basar. At the end of the children's story they each stood up, one at a time, and told what the story made them thankful for or some lesson they had learned from the story.

When the story ended, we all crowded to the center of the room, and parents placed hands on the heads of the children while they prayed in thanks for their little ones. Then it was time for the children to be put to bed. Yonadab explained to me that on Saturday nights the children are put to bed early so that the adults can have some uninterrupted time to break bread together.

Hemlah brought me a cup of mint tea, and I sat and talked with some of the women as people readied the rooms we had just occupied for the breaking of the bread. They spread colorful Nepalese tapestries on the walls and set futons on the floor to sit on. A low table occupied the middle of the room.

Only baptized members were allowed to participate in the intimate time of breaking bread. At this time, they shared what was on their hearts and had Communion together. They also ate a simple meal of soup with the bread and passed another cup of wine.

A special dinner was prepared for guests, which was eaten in another room (actually a separate house called the "Back House" because it was in back of the first). Another guest, Paul, and I shared dinner with Ehud, his wife, Nahala, and Kesher. Some of their older children, Deborah, Rivkah, and Suvav, served us, delivering each new course and waiting tables. I felt very honored and wished I could stay longer.

After the guest dinner and the breaking of the bread was concluded, everyone was to gather at the main house for tea, refreshments, and socializing. Very reluctantly, I left for home early to nurse Rachel and put her to bed. What remained with me was a feeling of fulfillment and satisfaction in having spent time fellowshiping with God and people who loved Him.

When I first went to The Community, I expected to find another "religion." But the more time I spent there, the clearer it became that this wasn't simply another religion, another way of viewing prophecy, or interpreting the Bible. The people I met are Christ-filled Christians; they are exuberant witnesses to the power of Christ in our lives on a day-to-day, hour-to-hour, minute-to-minute basis.

A visit to the synagogue

I next visited Rabbi Goldberg at the Rutland Jewish Center. He very kindly walked me through a mini-history lesson on Sabbath, emphasizing the Jewish perspective.

"In ancient days and early rabbinic days, the Jews observed the Sabbath and rested. There was not necessarily the concept of the Sabbath as a delight," Rabbi Goldberg said.

As Christians we might not necessarily thank the Pharisees for too much, but they were the ones responsible for instituting the idea that the Sabbath should be a delight. They read the Isaiah 58 passage: " 'If you call the Sabbath a delight . . .' " (Isaiah 58:13) and came to the conclusion that the Sabbath was not to be a day of deprivation. Rather than resting on the Sabbath, even if it killed you, they believed that if you were going to honor Sabbath and truly enjoy it, you needed physical enjoyment as well as spiritual enjoyment. You had to join the physical dimension with the spiritual in order to have a complete spirit and Sabbath. Part of the physical enjoyment they advocated was decent meals.

Because most people in ancient times were poor, they couldn't afford fancy meals. Their meals mostly consisted of a bread that was a cross between a pita and a matzah (having some leavening but not a true risen dough) and some beans. Even if they had to scrimp on daily meals, they were to have extra food for Sabbath. They were to have at least three good meals on the Sabbath, though emphasis was given to two: Friday evening and Sabbath afternoon.

Another important rabbinical mandate was that on the Sabbath one ought to have light. That meant that there were to be at least two oil lamps burning. Since most people did not have enough money for oil to burn lamps on a regular week night, they did not see each other very often.

The father, who was most often employed as a day laborer, would go out in the morning and try to get employment for the day. He would come home shortly before the sun set and give his wages to his wife. She hurried to the market and purchased enough flour and beans for supper. After she quickly prepared the food, the family would hastily eat it, most generally in the twilight. By the time they finished, it was dark, and they went to bed.

On Sabbath, because they had light, the family could eat more leisurely and spend some family time together before retiring for the night. They would talk and sing, having family fellowship. Most often they had no need of a fire on Sabbath, but during the cold season, as long as the fire was started before Sabbath and not tended, it was allowed to burn until it went out.[14]

In the sixth and seventh centuries, a major Jewish schism developed. A group called the Karaites (from the word kara meaning "those who read [the Bible]"*) formed. They believed and read only the Bible, ignoring any oral rabbinic interpretations of the Talmud. Neither the Karaites nor the Sadducees understood the Isaiah passage to mean that the Sabbath was to have any particular physical comforts. Their homes were cold and dark; their meals no more abundant on the Sabbath than any other day.

Today the typical Jewish wife has her cooking and cleaning done before Sabbath starts. She has the table set in readiness for the Sabbath, usually with a white tablecloth. There are two loaves of challah (a special white, sometimes braided, bread. You will find the recipe in chapter 9.) on the table, covered with a special challah cover or a napkin.

There are a couple reasons there are two loaves. One is that it is a reminder of the double portion of manna. Another is that the table

---

14. The Jews believe it is a sin to kindle (light) a fire on the Sabbath. They base this on Exodus 35:3. "You shall kindle no fire throughout your habitations on the Sabbath day." This stipulation has given rise to many creative ways to keep food (and water) hot for the duration of the Sabbath hours. Many homes have a hot water urn and keep hot plates beneath food that will be served hot Sabbath afternoon.

*Kara is translated "those who read"—the Bible is implied—as it is the only thing people reading in those days would have read.

is symbolic of the table of shewbread in the temple. It had six shelves, and on each shelf were two loaves of bread. The two loaves symbolize the top shelf of the table of shewbread.

The Sabbath candles are not usually on the table, although they are in the room where the meal is eaten, because once the lights are kindled they may not be moved. Should food spill on the tablecloth it would be impossible to change it for the Sabbath afternoon meal. There are always at least two candles. Some families light one additional candle for each child. Jewish rules dictate that once you light a certain amount of candles you are never to light any less. While you may increase in holiness, you are never to decrease.

Jewish women also use their best silverware and china. There is a wine glass at each place for the blessing of the wine. Some families have a knife (covered) on the table to cut the challah. Others do not because a knife symbolizes violence. If there is no knife, the family breaks the bread apart with their hands.

"Sabbath is the most important holy day and the most important holiday even though it comes every week," Rabbi Goldberg tells me.

The husband of the house and any sons go to the synagogue for the service which starts just before sundown. The wife will light the Sabbath candles at least eighteen minutes before sundown but no more than one and a half hours before. At this time, she will bless the candles. While saying the blessing, she moves her hands in circular motions over the candles (out and in, counterclockwise with the right hand, clockwise with the left). Although the blessing of the candles is the woman's duty, it is a man's responsibility to perform it if his wife is away, or if he doesn't have a wife, or if he is traveling.

I have given the phonetic Hebrew and its English counterpart for most of the following blessings. If they were too long, I stuck with the English.

Blessing for the Sabbath candles

BA-RUCH A-TA A-DO-NYE, EH-LO-HEY-NU MEH-LECH HA-O-LAM, A-SHER KI-D'SHA-NU B-MITS-VO-TAV V'TSI-VA-NU L'HAD-LIK NER SHEL SHA-BAT.

"Praised are You, Lord our God, King of the universe, Who has made us holy through Your commandments, and has commanded us to kindle the Sabbath lights."

While her husband is at the early Sabbath service, many Jewish wives will have their personal devotions or prayer to God. Once she has lit the candles, Sabbath has started for her and her household even though, technically, it is not yet Sabbath. The Jews observe Sabbath before it actually starts and after it actually ends.

When the husband and sons arrive home from services, it is time for dinner. The family gathers around the table, joins hands and sings a Sabbath hymn (usually one about the Sabbath angels). Then either the wife or the husband (or sometimes they take turns from week to week) blesses the children. When saying the blessing, the parent places his or her hands on the head of the child. There are three blessings. The first is recited over a son, the second over a daughter, and the third is recited over both sons and daughters.

Blessing of the children

To sons say:
Y'SIM'CHA EH-LO-HIM K'EF-RA-YIM V'CHI-M'NA-SHEH.

God grant that you grow to be like Joseph's sons, Ephraim and Manasseh.

To daughters say:

Y'SI-MECH EH-LO-HIM K'SA-RA, RIV-KA, RA-CHEL V'LEY-A

"God grant that you grow to be like the mothers of our people: Sarah, Rebecca, Rachel and Leah."

To both sons and daughters say:

Y-VA-REH-CH'CHA A-DO-NYE V'YISH-M'REH-CHA. YA-ER A-DO-NYE PA-NAV EY-LEH-CHA VI-CHU-NEH-KA. YI-SA A-DO-NYE PA-NAV EY-LEH-CHA, V'YA-SEM L'CHA SHA-LOM.

"May the Lord bless you and watch over you. May the Lord's presence shine upon you and bestow kindness upon you. May the Lord's presence favor you and bring you peace."

After this blessing, the husband blesses his wife.

Husband to Wife

What a rare find is a capable wife! Her worth is far beyond that of rubies.

Her husband puts his confidence in her and lacks no good thing.

She is good to him, never bad, all the days of her life.

She performs her task with vigor . . . , and stretches her hands out to the needy. . . .

She is clothed with strength and splendor; she looks to the future cheerfully.

Her mouth is full of wisdom, her tongue with kindly teaching.

Her children declare her happy; her husband praises her.
"Many women have done well, but you surpass them all."
Grace is deceptive and beauty is illusory; it is for her reverence for the Lord that a woman is to be praised.

And then the wife blesses her husband.

Wife to Husband

Happy is the man who has reverence for the Lord, who is ardently devoted to His commandments.

His descendants will be mighty in the land, a blessed generation of righteous people.

Wealth and riches will be in his house, his righteousness lasting forever.

A light shines for the upright in the darkness . . . he shall never be shaken.

He shall enjoy the fruit of his labors; he shall be happy and prosper.

His wife shall be like a fruitful vine . . . ; his children like olive saplings around his table. . . .

May the Lord bless you from Zion; may you share the prosperity of Jerusalem all the days of your life and live to see your children's children.

May all be well with Israel!

The Kiddush is a prayer proclaiming the holiness of Sabbath, usually recited over a cup of wine (or grape juice). If there is no wine or grape juice, certain bread products can be substituted. The first part of the Kiddush is Genesis 2:1-3:

Kiddush

"The heaven and earth were finished, and all their array. On the seventh day God finished the work which he had been doing, and he ceased on the seventh day from all the work that He had done. God blessed the seventh day and declared it holy, because on it God ceased from all the work of creation which He had done."

BA-RUCH A-TA A-DO-NYE EH-LO-HEY-NU MEH-LECH HA-O-LAM, BO-REY PREE HA-GA-FEN.

"Praised are you, Lord our God, King of the universe, Creator of the fruit of the vine."

BA-RUCH A-TA A-DO-NYE, EH-LO-HEY-NU MEH-LECH HA-O-LAM, A-SHER KI-D'SHA-NU B'MITS-VO-TAV V'RA-TSA VA-NU, V'SHA-BAT KOD-SHO B'A-HA'VA U-V'RA-TSON HIN-CHEE-LA-NU, ZI-KA-RON L'MA-A-SEY V'REY-SHEET, KEE-HU YOM T'CHEE-LA L'MIK-RA-EŸ KO-DESH, ZEY-CHER LEE-TSEE-AT MITS-RA-YIM. KEE VA-NU VA-CHAR-TA, V'O-TA-NU KI-DASH-TA MI-KOL HA-A-MEEM, V'SHA-BAT KOD-SH'CHA B-A-HA-VA U-V'RA-TSON HIN-CHAL-TA-NU. BA-RUCH A-TA A-DO-NYE, M'KA-DESH HA-SHA-BAT.

"Praised are You, Lord our God, King of the universe, Who has made us holy through His commandments and has been pleased with us. You have lovingly granted us the gift of Your holy Sabbath as our inheritance, a reminder of creation and the first of our sacred days, recalling the Exodus from Egypt. You have taken delight in us and have consecrated us from among all peoples, giving us Your holy Sabbath as our heritage. Praised are You, Lord, Who endows the Sabbath with holiness."

Next the hands are washed ceremonially. "This is not for cleanliness," Rabbi Goldberg tells me. "For that you should use soap and water. This is merely pouring water over the hands. For this we use a special cup with two handles. You pour water over the right, then the left and then the right again." The blessing is recited while washing or while drying the hands.

Washing of the hands

BA-RUCH A-TA A-DO-NYE, EH-LO-HEY-NU MEH-LECH HA-O-LAM, A-SHER KI-D'SHA-NU B'MITS-VO-TAV, V'TSI-VA-NU AL N'TEE-LAT YA-DA-YIM.

The family is to remain quiet from this point until the bread has been blessed and distributed and a piece eaten and swallowed. The husband takes the bread, holding the loaves one on top of the other while he recites the blessing. Then he cuts off or tears off an end and distributes a piece to each family member. They sprinkle salt on it.

The reason for salt is that the Pharisees created the modern Jewish Sabbath. The members of the family are like members of the priesthood and should observe many of the laws that apply to the priests. They should treat the table with honor and dignity as the priests would the altar in the temple. The meal is to be eaten as though it were a sacred meal as the priests would have eaten their portion of the sacrifices in God's presence. That is the reason the hands are washed, because the priests wouldn't approach the altar without washing their hands to remove the defilement from unsacred things.

The sacrifices were offered with salt. Salt gives flavor. It is also the symbol of longevity.

"All the heave offerings of the holy things, which the children of Israel offer to the Lord, I have given to you and your sons and daughters with you as an ordinance forever; it is a covenant of salt forever before the Lord with you and your descendants with you" (Numbers 18:19, NKJV).

"Should you not know that the Lord God of Israel gave the dominion over Israel to David forever, to him and his sons, by a covenant of salt?" (2 Chronicles 13:5, NKJV).

Blessing for the Sabbath bread

BA-RUCH A-TA A-DO-NYE, EH-LO-HEY-NU MEH-LECH HA-O-LAM, HA-MO-TSEE LEH-CHEM MIN HA-A-RETS.
"Praised are You, Lord our God, King of the universe, Who brings forth our bread from the earth."

After the bread is blessed, dinner is served. Between courses the family will sing Sabbath table songs. This is an old tradition dating back to the fifth and sixth century. Some of the songs are in Hebrew and some in Aramaic. They are songs in honor of the Sabbath, God, and Sabbath practices and customs. The Hebrew word for these songs is *zemirot*, which means "songs" but is understood to mean Sabbath Table songs. These songs are sung at all Sabbath meals.

Grace is said after meals. It is considered even more important than grace before meals. "An ancient sage said 'If you do not say grace before meals it is like stealing,' " Rabbi Goldberg said. "But, to say grace after meals is considered a commandment because it is written in the Torah."

"When you have eaten and are full, then you shall bless the Lord your God for the good land which He has given you" (Deuteronomy 8:10, NKJV).

The actual grace after meals is much longer than this, and the English translation is shorter than the Hebrew version, so I have printed here only the English part. The husband can say the whole thing, or the wife and husband can alternate. (Or for our purposes, older children can participate as well.)

Grace after meals

"Praised are You, Lord our God, King of the universe, Who sustains the whole world in His goodness. In His grace and love He provides for all living beings. His love is endless. May it be Your will that we never lack food, for You surely provide sufficient nourishment for all. Indeed You deal generously with all whom You have created. Praised are You, Lord, Who feeds us all."

"We praise you, Lord our God, for You are our divine Father and glorious King, our holy Creator and Redeemer. You are the Shepherd of Israel, Who every day acts with kindness to all, and we pray that You will never deprive us of Your goodness."

"May our merciful Father bring us to that time which will always be Sabbath and ever restful."

"May He who made the harmony of all the heavens bring peace and harmony to us, to all Israel, and to all the world."

After the meal is over, the Jewish family relaxes, sings, talks, or plays quiet games. There is a later service they may attend. The dishes used on Friday night are washed because they will be needed the next day. However, dishes from the Sabbath lunch meal are washed after Sabbath.

"Washing the dishes on Sabbath which won't be used until the first day of the week or until the following Sabbath would be working on the Sabbath for a week day," Rabbi Goldberg said. "But, to wash dishes on Sabbath that must be reused on Sabbath is permitted."

Saturday morning, the family will eat a nominal breakfast, which does not involve bread, and then go to the synagogue for services. Following services, the Sabbath afternoon meal repeats the same pattern from the Kiddush on. It will also include table songs.

Following the meal, the family might take a nap (although it is not considered desirable to sleep away the Sabbath) or take a walk or play games. "Members of my congregation will ask me what is an appropriate activity for Sabbath," Rabbi Goldberg told me. "And there are some activities which in themselves are not forbidden, but which can take over so completely that while you participate in them you forget that it is Sabbath.

"My own criteria for determining whether or not an activity is suitable for Sabbath is to ask three questions.

1. Does it promote rest and or relaxation?
2. Does it bring delight and enjoyment?
3. Does it give you a sense of holiness and sanctity? In other words, does it add to your sense of Sabbath?

"If it fits all three, it is a most desirable activity. If it fits one or two, it is questionable. Whatever you do on the Sabbath day, you should never forget that it is Sabbath. If an activity causes you to forget that it is Sabbath then that activity is not in the spirit of the Sabbath."

Sabbath is officially over, not at sundown, but when you can see three stars in the sky. Then Jews have the Havdolah ceremony. For this they use three things: a candle with many wicks, sweet-smelling spices (like stick cinnamon and cloves), and a glass of wine or grape juice. The candle is lighted first. The purpose of many wicks is to have a bright light. On the first day of creation, God created light. So the bright light symbolizes the light on the first day of creation.

Then they spill some of the wine or grape juice into a saucer and snuff out the candle in the wine. This symbolizes the hope that you have plenty in the week ahead (if you have enough wine or grape juice to spill, you have plenty). And they smell the spices, which symbolize the remembered sweetness of the Sabbath. These are kept in a spice box or container. The aroma of the Sabbath should remain with you through the week ahead. Then they say a prayer separating the holiness of the Sabbath from the rest of the week.

CHAPTER
6

Celebration
Suggestions

OK, so now what? Maybe you've seen, like I have, that there really is a lot more potential to the Sabbath that we aren't taking advantage of. But, maybe, like me, you don't really know where to start. Should you design a whole celebration regime and institute it next Sabbath? Or should you take the bits and pieces you like and stick them in here and there?

First, a word of advice. Breaking out of a rut or a routine is not easy. There is a great deal of discomfort involved. Hopefully, there is also a good share of excitement as well. If you think that your Sabbath celebration is lacking some joy and, well, celebration, it is best to start small. Try incorporating one thing. Choose one new aspect of celebrating the Sabbath that you feel the most comfortable with and start there.

When introducing anything new, it is best to begin small and work up rather than to immerse yourself and give up when it seems overwhelming. That may sound simple, but many exercise programs, diet reforms, and New Year's resolutions get dumped every year because they are too grandiose. Don't let conviction urge you to take on too much at once. Remember that the *spirit* of celebrating is more important than the vehicle you choose to celebrate with.

In chapter 7, we'll work through some questions and suggestions that will help you design a plan for celebrating the Sabbath and give tips for incorporating the new with the established. Right now, I'd like to concentrate on some specific things you may want to consider when you get to chapter 7.

I remember my formal wedding. (I make the distinction because it is a little known fact that Rob and I eloped on Valentine's Day in 1985. We had a formal wedding the following August for our family and friends because they wouldn't go for our idea of a small outdoor ceremony in the meadow where we'd gotten engaged.) Months went into the preparation of gown, ceremony, reception, music, dresses, attendants, pictures, and decorations. I was driven to the stone church in my grandfather's long white New Yorker, but we arrived too early.

Cars jammed the narrow town streets, and people converged on the church anticipating the wedding. Rob, who wasn't supposed to see me, was outside placing the just-delivered flowers with their recipients. I got out but made a conspicuous sight dressed in a handmade wedding gown with a train that rivaled Princess Diana's. My uncle David rushed to my aid, carrying my massive train so I could duck behind some cars and wait for the guests and Rob to enter the church before I did.

I still remember how I felt hiding behind those cars. I was eight years old again, hiding behind the garage playing hide-and-seek, my skin prickling with excitement, my stomach in knots of anxiety. It was exhilarating and terrifying at the same time. Finally, everyone was safely inside and Uncle David carried my train as we walked into the church. It was a beautiful wedding, and we have pictures to prove it.

I can't imagine what my wedding would have been like if I had only shown up as I was scheduled to walk up the aisle or say my vows. Even our elopement, decided about four days before the event, took some planning. And you can be sure I wasn't schlepping around nonchalantly until it was time to drive over to the justice of the peace. No, I was getting everything "just so": my hair, my dress, my face.

Anticipation is an integral part of any celebration and, conversely, anything worth celebrating is going to generate anticipation. Our anticipation of the Sabbath celebration will ensure that we don't "infringe" on the Sabbath hours with worldly pursuits. Anticipation will prompt us to gather *before* the sun actually sets rather than after.

Some of the things we do to anticipate the Sabbath are done throughout Preparation Day, or Friday. These include cleaning, cooking, praying. Others can serve as "signals" to family members that Sabbath is coming. An example of this can be taken from Kashruth, or kosher cooking.

Kashruth is the Hebrew noun formed from the same root as the more familiar adjective, kosher, which means "fit to eat." Kashruth, then, is the system developed to determine such fitness. While the system of Kashruth is relatively straightforward and can be explained to any reasonable person in a matter of minutes, there are various elements that complicate it. For our purposes, I will simply point out the basis of the system, which is that it consists of those foods deemed kosher and their preparation. As well, meat and dairy products are never mixed in a single meal. Any meal, therefore, is either a meat or a dairy meal.

Since the fundamental force of kashruth is to circumscribe the role of flesh in cuisine, the meat meal is a potent affair and what might be called its meatness stays in force even after diners get up from the table. Observant Jews wait as long as six hours after a meat meal before eating dairy foods again. Few people wait this long, but some interval is necessary. After a dairy meal, however, no wait (some people wait an hour) is required before it is permissible to eat meat again (unless the dairy meal included hard cheeses), but *it is customary to signal the changeover, perhaps by changing the tablecloth* [15] (emphasis mine).

This custom of signaling a changeover is something we can adopt for our Sabbath celebrations. There are many simple things that can signal a changeover in the household. But, these things, in order for them to retain their full significance, must be set aside for Sabbath use only. This doesn't have to mean added expense, because many of the things that can signal the changeover are already in your house!

For example, you can put out clean towels, change bed sheets, put flowers on the table, or reserve a particular tablecloth for Sabbath use. Children can have special toys they play with only on Sabbath. These simple things can be very effective tools to foster anticipation.

When I change the beds on Friday morning, I also put out what I call my Sabbath bedspreads. These are the nicest ones I have. My son ran into my bedroom one Friday morning, looked at the bedspread, and exclaimed, "Yeeeah! It's Sabbath today!" He knew what that bedspread meant. Each bed in the house has a Sabbath bedspread. That way, every child sees a marked difference in his or her bedroom during the holy hours. These bedspreads come off Sunday morning. [16]

---

15. *The Jewish American Kitchen*, 17, 18.
16. *Oh No, It's Sabbath Again and I'm Not Ready!*, 87.

Besides creating anticipation for the Sabbath, changeover signals are also the seeds of traditions that once planted will grow strong as you nurture them. Traditions are important because they anchor us. Temporal things may change, life may get rocky, situations may be uncomfortable, but traditions provide a sense of security and continuity in life.

In an interview for *Women of Spirit,* Jo Ann Davidson was asked how she made Sabbath more than a doctrine for her children. She said:

You know, as an adult I enjoy reading and thinking about the theological aspects of the Sabbath, but that's not appealing to kids. One key to making Sabbath inviting is to make it appeal to all their senses. And so when the kids were little I made a real effort to have their favorite foods on Sabbath.

All week long I taught the kids nutrition with their meals. But Sabbath I just cooked their favorites that made the house smell good too. And for the sense of sight we had fresh flowers and candlelight.

The sense of touch is important too, so on Friday nights we'd give the kids back rubs as we put them to bed. We were coming home very late one Friday night and they said, "Mom, it's late, isn't it?" Yes, it was.

"Is there time for back rubs?"

So we had back rubs even though it was late, so Sabbaths would *feel* good.

Then there's the sense of hearing. On Friday nights Dick and I got into the habit of playing the piano and singing after we put them to bed. Not that we sing that well, but they'd go to sleep to the sound of Christian hymns. It's been so rewarding to me, because through this they grew to love the grand hymns.[17]

Involving the senses in celebrating the Sabbath is a powerful thing. Our most powerful memories are linked to sensory experience. For example, what do you think of when you smell freshly cut grass? Hear a choir sing? Eat by candlelight? The list is practically endless. Advertisers, marketing personnel, and solicitors know that if they can tap into our emotions, they can manipulate us to buy or give. By the same token, we can use our emotions to solidify our foundation and enhance our Sabbath experience.

So sundown approaches, and you gather the family together, or you and your spouse get together to begin to welcome the Sabbath. Now what?

Before the setting of the sun let the members of the family assemble *to read God's word, to sing and pray.* There is need of reform here, for many have been remiss. We need to confess to God and to one another. We should begin anew to make special arrangements that every member of the family may be prepared to honor the day which God has blessed and sanctified[18] (emphasis mine).

Read God's Word. Sing. Pray. Simple enough, right? When reading the Bible, you might want to consider the ages and spiritual maturity of your audience. A group of adults might love the old language and majesty of the King James Version or New King

17. Jo Ann Davidson, "Creating Sabbath Delight," *Women of Spirit*, Penny Estes Wheeler, May/June 1997.
18. *Testimonies for the Church*, 6:356, 357.

James Version, but it isn't very practical for children.

A group diverse in spiritual maturity might enjoy reading a newer version such as Eugene Peterson's The Message translations or the Everyday Bible. Both of these read in a more contemporary fashion. They aren't especially suited to in-depth study but put a wonderful spin on familiar concepts. For households with children, there are many great Bible storybooks from toddlers to beginners to preschoolers and right on up. In a family mix with children and adults, you might consider a chapter from a contemporary version and one from a children's Bible.

Little ones could be provided with crayons and Bible story coloring books to keep them occupied during the adult reading. Or, if it is too hard to concentrate and keep the children quiet, the adults could save their study time together for after the children are in bed.

Singing can be as involved and exciting or as sedate as you want it to be. Whether you choose to sing hymns, spiritual campfire songs, or Cradle Roll favorites, everyone can participate in making music to the Lord. It doesn't matter if you have a piano to gather around or even a guitar player. What matters is that you have the heart to make music. Even if you are musically challenged, you can shake a tambourine or tap your feet.

A worthy investment, particularly if you have young children, is a collection of rhythm instruments. These don't have to be elaborate either. You can make many of them: sandpaper blocks (wooden blocks with sandpaper glued or stapled on), drums (made out of Crisco cans or oatmeal containers), jingle bells (bells sewn onto bands of ribbon), shakers (made out of anything that can hold dried beans). Children will like kazoos made from the cardboard tube inside a toilet paper roll. Cut out a square of wax paper and fasten it over one end of the tube with a rubber band. Put your lips around the open end and hum.

Pray. Keep prayers simple. I remember my family's attempts to have family worship when I was little. Praying was tedious. We knelt, straight up, on wooden floors, for what seemed like hours. I would rock back and forth from one knee to the other when the pain got to be too much. Forcing your children to endure long-winded prayer sessions is not going to instill them with a sense of celebration.

Pray succinctly. Let your children pray. Before you begin you might want to talk about the people whom you are praying for and let each child choose one to remember in prayer. Or use sentence prayers to keep prayers manageable. Each person prays one sentence at a time. If this is a new concept, older children might be self-conscious and need some encouragement. However, this method will introduce children to public prayer in small doses in a controlled and supportive environment.

At family worship let the children take a part. Let all bring their Bibles and each read a verse or two. Then let some familiar hymn be sung, followed by prayer. For this, Christ has given a model. The Lord's Prayer was not intended to be repeated merely as a form, but it is an illustration of what our prayers should be - simple, earnest, and comprehensive. In a simple petition tell the Lord your needs and express gratitude for His mercies. Thus you invite Jesus as a welcome guest into your home and heart. In the family long prayers concerning remote objects are not in place. They make the hour of prayer a weariness, when it should be regarded as a privilege and blessing. Make the season one of interest and joy. [19]

19.Ibid., 358.

It's hard for those of us who grew up with rigid family worship to come to terms with the idea that it can be *fun*. But nowhere in His Word does God say that worship has to be boring.

If you ever sat through dry worship times as a child when your parents dragged you to the family altar and pounded biblical training into your bored head, you know why it is so important for worship to be a time children look forward to rather than one they dread.

It is too easy to miss the point of religious training with children. There is so much to teach them that you can forget to stress the *love relationship* with God. After all, the other things are demonstrable: Don't lie, love your neighbors, be nice to pets, do unto others all the good things you want them to do unto you. Developing their relationship with a Person they can't see is more difficult and requires more attention.

As I write these words, people everywhere are getting ready to celebrate Christmas. Millions of little children are preparing for a visit from a mythical figure named Santa Claus. Here's a guy who does all sorts of impossible things, but they believe in him. Setting aside the issue of whether or not this is detrimental to children's faith, let's focus on the *belief* that's going on here and how it's fostered.

Children love Santa. Why? Because he brings them things. School teachers and day-care providers have told me that Christmas celebrations at school and in day-care centers begin weeks ahead of time because children love Christmas. Why? Santa.

Parents and other adults in positions of trust plant, encourage, and nurture the person of Santa. How? By reminding children that he is coming and when. By reminding children that they must be good so they will be rewarded. By singing songs about Santa and telling stories and making lists. Santa is so appealing to children that they *want* to believe in him even if they know he doesn't exist and don't receive any Santa-related hype.

Our son, Josh, is four and a half this year. He knows there is no Santa, and we don't encourage Santa in any way. But even he has picked up enough so that he knows who Santa is and wonders if *maybe* he might drop some presents down the chimney, even though I've shown him where the presents are, all wrapped and waiting to be put under a tree when we get one. Still, he *wants* to think there is someone out there who will be bringing him lots of lovely gifts.

Of course it is relatively simple to capture the interest of children for one month. Maybe Santa's popularity wouldn't be so dramatic if he were around the other eleven months of the year. But the fact remains that there are many little children who believe he exists. Why? Because their parents and other authority figures say he does and they have proof; he brings them presents.

Is it easy for little children to believe? Yes. And we can use that eagerness to our advantage when teaching our children about Jesus as our Savior and about the weekly gift of the Sabbath. They don't have to wait twelve months for one day of gifts that will be forgotten or broken a week later. They can receive a gift of eternal value every week! It doesn't require batteries and "one size fits all." Isn't that exciting?

Now that you have some ideas for signaling a changeover from the work week to the Sabbath day and have read some suggestions for opening the Sabbath, let's talk about the Sabbath day itself. If you are accustomed to participating in "lay activities"—i.e., the Sabbath afternoon nap—you are in for a treat. Yes, the Sabbath is meant to be for us physical rest, but that's not all. It was also meant for our mental rest and for our spiritual rest.

It was meant for our *renewal*. And it's hard to get too renewed when you are sawing logs. I'm not saying that naps on Sabbath are wrong. But I *am* saying that if your entire Sabbath experience consists of going to church and sleeping the afternoon away, you are missing a great deal.

In pleasant weather let parents walk with their children in the fields and groves. Amid the beautiful things of nature tell them the reason for the institution of the Sabbath. Describe to them God's great work of creation. Tell them that when the earth came from His hand, it was holy and beautiful. Every flower, every shrub, every tree, answered the purpose of its Creator. Everything upon which the eye rested was lovely and filled the mind with thoughts of the love of God. Every sound was music in harmony with the voice of God. Show that it was sin which marred God's perfect work; that thorns and thistles, sorrow and pain and death, are all the result of disobedience to God. Bid them see how the earth, though marred with the curse of sin, still reveals God's goodness. The green fields, the lofty trees, the glad sunshine, the clouds, the dew, the solemn stillness of the night, the glory of the starry heavens, and the moon in its beauty all bear witness of the Creator. Not a drop of rain falls, not a ray of light is shed on our unthankful world, but it testifies to the forbearance and love of God.[20]

What a great way to spend Sabbath!

One of the nice things about Sabbath celebration is that in order to celebrate, you really only need precisely two people, you and God. If your family doesn't want to participate or your spouse could care

---

20. Ibid., 358.

less, that doesn't mean that you have to miss out on the blessing and joy of the Sabbath.

There is a place you can celebrate and share your Sabbath joy even if there's not another soul around to share it with. The concept of journals is hardly new. Remember those diaries with the little locks that your brother always managed to pick so he could read who liked whom and tease you unmercifully? Girls usually start those, but that doesn't mean men can't or shouldn't journal.

Journaling, despite what you might think, is not hard. The *habit* of journaling takes some practice. But your goal here isn't to write volumes of journals like Thoreau. It's to record your observations about the Sabbath or about God, maybe from things God has shown you through the week and brought to mind now as you contemplate holy subjects.

And as my friend Baird says, you can write a lot of ways, but you can't write wrong. If you aren't happy with your writing style, simply make lists at first. Prayer requests, answers to prayer, and points of interest in your Bible study are good topics to cover. Once you are comfortable with that, write a little about what God has shown you during the week or how you have gained victory in areas of your life that you have been struggling with.

Try not to make your journal a list of grievances or a place to dwell on failure. I've kept a journal off and on since I was fourteen, but as I go back through it, I see the same depressing thread running through each entry. I always journaled through my problems and rarely journaled about things I had learned or what I thought about any other topics.

Concentrate on positive subjects and progress. Read back over it often to remind yourself of where you have come from and how God has worked in your life. Trace the spiritual growth. There are bound to be some down days captured in your journals, just as there are down days in our spiritual journey. But don't get caught there. Move on to greater growth and insight.

When you are comfortable with journaling, consider adding the element of illustration to your words. You don't have to be an artist to make sketches in your journal. The term I've heard used to describe this type of journaling is the "illuminated" journal. One of the most appealing aspects of sketching in a journal to me is that in order to sketch something, no matter how crudely, you must pay attention to it.

The way we live restricts the amount of attention we can pay to details like a sunset washed in orange or a single new leaf on a tree or a cloudy sky. Getting out into nature is great, but recording it on paper is even better. Even if your sketches are horrible, you will still take from this exercise a newfound respect for the things that God has created.

Families can create a Blessings Box. A Blessings Box can be made out of any kind of box, and children should be encouraged to help in whatever way they can. Use a box that has a lid and cover the bottom and top separately with wrapping paper so you can take the top off the box without ruining the wrapping.

Cut a hole in the top of the box so you can put in slips of paper. You might want to purchase a special small notepad and glue it onto the side of the box so paper will always be handy. Likewise, you can tie a pen to a string and then attach it to the box. That way no one has an excuse for not recording a blessing!

During the week, each family member who receives a blessing or an answer to prayer writes it down on a slip of paper and puts it into the Blessings Box. At the Friday evening meal, one person (family members can take turns either by the Sabbath or by the slip of paper) reads the slips of paper out loud. Allow time for discussion and praise of each blessing.

Another great way for families to celebrate the Sabbath is to choose a Bible story to dramatize on Friday evening. It could be the story that the children have been reading each day for worship from their Sabbath School quarterlies, or, if they are older, let them choose a story each week and play the parts. Make this a real event by popping popcorn and rigging up costumes and props as well as you can.

This is a particularly great activity for winter Friday nights as Sabbath starts so much earlier than in the summer. Invited guests will enjoy the play and can even be called upon to take a part in a pinch. And you don't have to have children to do this. A creative couple can take the Bible story and put their own spin on it, maybe acting out only the dialogue.

Celebrations in diverse places

There's no doubt about it. Celebrations can take place anywhere. You can be alone under an umbrella in a downpour or in the middle of a crush of people at New Year's. The spirit is what counts because you can also be in either of those places and be as lonely and miserable as you please.

This is a very important point because there are bound to be times when you are stuck somewhere far from home and the Sabbath arrives. What do you do? Skip the celebration simply because you are not home in familiar territory surrounded by all your Sabbath finery and tradition?

No, of course not.

Because the *spirit* of the celebration and the *Spirit* of the Sabbath will be there with you. That is why it is so important to have those elements present in your weekly Sabbath celebration. When you strip Sabbath down to its essence, it is still as powerful and as awesome as it was on display. You can *celebrate* Sabbath with nothing more than yourself.

Of course, if you are going to be traveling over the Sabbath, it will be necessary to make some plans ahead of time. Rabbi Goldberg related to me what happens when a Jewish family travels. They plan to stop at their hotel several hours before Sabbath will begin so they can set up everything ahead of time.

"In a Jewish family, if it's not done before the Sabbath it's not done," Rabbi Goldberg said when I asked about what happens if you didn't get around to something beforehand. "You must plan ahead. For the observant minded this is not a problem or a hassle."

The women have traveling candlesticks, which fold up, and they bring the food they will need in coolers. Any food that needs to be hot, they will set up on hot plates. As he talked about these things, it occurred to me that it would be an excellent idea to have a Sabbath travel kit.

The best thing would be for this kit to have items for celebrating the Sabbath, which would be set aside for traveling only. That way you would be sure that you had the things you needed when you needed them. This could be stored inside your suitcase when you weren't traveling.

Most Adventists would have no problem with eating at a restaurant on Friday night, provided they reached the restaurant before Sabbath. Many would feel fine about eating there even after Sabbath started, as long as their check was paid for beforehand. And still others would have no compunctions about eating at a restaurant and paying for it during the Sabbath.

But wouldn't it make Sabbath much more special to have your meal prepared ahead of time and brought with you, in your room where you could worship your God and welcome His Sabbath as you could never do in a public place like a restaurant? Most of us do not travel so frequently that this extra preparation would become a nuisance or be completely impractical.

Making the Sabbath hours common by infringing on them with work or being in a secular place thinking about secular things is like devaluing a gift. In this case, it is a precious gift. Not one minute of it should be wasted.

Passing the torch

Children who participate with their families in a Sabbath celebration will miss it when they go to live on their own, begin their own families, or go away to school. Here is where parents can provide necessary guidance and support so the beautiful blessing of Sabbath passes from one generation to the next.

As your son or daughter prepares to leave home, talk to them about past Sabbaths and their plans for future Sabbaths. Because they have grown up in your house, they have been a participant in *your* Sabbath celebration. Now they are facing a celebration of their own. Help them to create it.

A wonderful gift for a child leaving home is a basket or nice box full of Sabbath celebration items: candles, candlesticks, white linen tablecloth, challah cloth, havdolah candle, spice box, wine goblet (one if they are single, two if they are getting married), and other items that have become important in your celebrations. If they are accustomed to having fresh flowers on their Sabbath table, include a gift certificate to a florist.

Don't forget recipes. Include a batch of recipes for their favorite Sabbath foods and any special ingredients, such as spices, they will need to get them started. Even more important than this, of course, is teaching them how to cook in the first place!

I don't know if the kids growing up today are much different from kids when I was growing up. I think the problems are basically the same. We just come up with fancier names for them. But one thing I do know is that kids will not blindly accept what you have to offer. If you don't explain to them why you do things the way you do them or if they can't see your principles in your life, they will not embrace your God or your religion when they are out of your sphere of influence.

The best, most basic, essential heritage you can give your children is Jesus Christ. If He is on your lips but not in your heart, your children will have a much tougher time finding Him and relating to Him. They may just decide He isn't worth it. And that would be tragic.

One way to anchor them in Him is to show them the true celebration of Sabbath. Show them Sabbath the way it was meant to be. Show them that the Sabbath is a delight and then help them make the transition from your home to one of their own.

Sabbath in the city

This chapter was supposed to end here, but I asked a few friends to read this manuscript and give me their opinion on it. One of those friends was Lena, who lives in the Bronx, New York. She e-mailed me with her comments and added, "Now all you have to do is one called 'Sabbath Keeping for the City Dwellers.'" So, I asked her what she meant, how Sabbath was different in the city, and this is what she told me.

"Well, according to my girlfriend Michelle, whose mom heaps down fire and brimstones on her head every Friday, because that's when she chooses to do her cleaning—it shouldn't matter that we live in the city. Geography is not an excuse. That's just the problem, we city dwellers have too many excuses. We don't place too much emphasis on the Sabbath because we think that God would under-stand the subway, the overtime, the distraction, etc. City dwellers focus primarily on the job, money, and advancement. So the un-winding really never comes for us. We talk about the job at lunch, on the way home, and when we get home.

"We are surrounded with the drive to survive. The reminders are on the pavement in the form of a homeless person or a beggar on the subway. There is no God to see or reflect on. The surburbans get a glimpse of God when they look out the train window and see trees or the deer that come into their backyards. But the urban dwellers have to worry about if they are going to make it in one piece on the elevator ride to their floors. God is with them then, because it's 'Please, God, just let me get in my door.'

"We are open to so many more temptations. No time to stop and think. Everything is right in your face. In the isolated areas there is a pause because there is quiet. Outside of the city you are surrounded by God, whether it's in the trees, the grass, or the creative noises—the wind or even birds. I can watch the squirrels play, but in the back of my mind, I remember that I'm not supposed to get close to them. The concrete jungle suffocates creation.

"I know that all of this seems strange, but it is so real. The Enoch walk has to be constant in the city. Sabbath should be Sabbath every-where and every time, but it just seems that with us city dwellers it is like being diabetic and living in a house made of sugar. The neigh-bors next door choose to play their music the loudest on Friday nights. Irritating rhythms pulsating through your doors distract you from your spiritual concentration. Because you have been hearing those same sounds all week, you might even start singing along or rocking to it. It's the subliminal seduction of it all. It's more draining because we allow ourselves to get caught up.

"Granted, all we play in our house is Christian music; it's a different story when you walk out of the sanctuary of your home. We city dwellers are full of excuses. Michelle said she would stop her Friday meditation because she wanted to see why the police helicopters were buzzing inches from the balcony of her co-op apartment. Then she'd forget to return because she wanted to know what they were looking for next to the Adventist church down the road. The distractions are the excuses we use. We are accustomed to too much excitement—too much entertainment. No time to think. The city life does not allow us the peace of pausing.

"When you talk about 'The Community,' I wish our church service was like that. In the city, Sabbath is another work day. Really, the only rest we get is on Sunday. Isn't that so twisted? Sabbath School is a joke—not enough time to get our thoughts together. The in-between is pure business and meeting announcements. Friday night is choir practice. To me, that is the ultimate perversity. No one wants to take time away from their jobs or evenings to meet in the week for business meetings or practice. But Friday, the start of the Sabbath, is just perfect for everyone.

"My niece is 14, and she gets home from youth choir practice at about 11:00 p.m. on Friday night. After divine service there are announcements for this meeting and that. Sabbath is harder on us city dwellers because we treat it as just another work day."

I'm sure that, like me, you can identify with parts of what Lena is saying, even if you don't live in a city. Rutland, where I live, is the second largest city in Vermont (yes, that's a state) but, compared to *real* cities like New York or Seattle, it's not much more than a pitstop in the landscape. And I don't even live in the city; I live just outside it. During the half of the year when there are leaves on the trees, I can't even see my nearest neighbors, let alone hear them. The only noise I hear comes from my children (and occasionally the dogs).

So, you might ask—and with good reason—what on earth could I possibly contribute to Lena's or any city dweller's problem with keeping Sabbath in the city. But it just so happens that I am a whiz at solving other people's problems. Also, I spent six months or so living in the town of St. Johnsbury in what was, for a country bumpkin, considered big city life.

The question of noise in the city is probably the biggest obstacle to Sabbath peace. In the city, you can't just escape from the noise. You're trapped with it. Really, you have three options.

1. You can create your own noise. Put on headphones with relaxing Christian music or soothing recordings of waterfalls, rain, or nature sounds. Everyone has heard of the stereotypical teenager who blocks out life with headphones. Why can't it work the same way for a good purpose? If the noise around you isn't too bad, try turning your stereo on and play nature sounds or soft Christian music. Get a fountain. It's amazing how calming the sound of running water can be.

2. Escape it. When Jesus wanted to rest, He got away from the crowds and the noise. I can't think of a city, or even town, that doesn't have a botanical garden, park, or some safe place where people have tried to reclaim the earth. Obviously you don't want to flee from your apartment every Friday night, but when it gets really bad, consider this as an option. Bring your worship to the park, playground, or fountain. You may be surrounded by concrete, but above you is God's sky.

"Sometimes," says Lena, "we go to the park on Sabbath afternoons to 'Interpret God' in the images we see. We walk around and observe and then meet again to relate the things we saw in nature that spoke to us about God."

3. Get support. If you live in the city and your friends live in the city, chances are they're facing the same problems with noise and distractions that you are. Get together and face it together. You'll be less distracted by what's outside your walls if you have good friends to strengthen you *inside* your walls. If you don't want to have to clean your apartment enough for company every weekend, take turns. Rotate the Friday night meeting at different people's houses. Or if your church doesn't object and it's located in a better (translate: quieter) place, gather there. Maybe there is a room available that you could decorate to look homey. People who want to can come and worship together.

Which brings me to Lena's next point, about our worship services being so much work. I think our culture has conditioned us to expect entertainment. We're not too far short of being issued those big white cards with black numbers like the Olympic judges that we can hold up after the parts of the worship program to score the participants. There's a long-standing joke about going home after church and carving up the preacher for dinner. Sadly, there's a lot of truth to that. But the preacher isn't the only one to suffer. Anyone contributing to the "entertainment" is fair game.

Please don't misunderstand me. There are folks who work awfully hard coming up with fantastic, inspiring, faith-challenging programs for Sabbath School and worship service. I know. I'm one of them. All I'm saying is, don't put the entertainment value above the worship experience.

I'm *not* suggesting any organization for a Friday night get-together. In fact, I'd go so far as to boldly suggest staying away from any organized program at all. I think it's a terrible handicap to not be able to get together as Christians and just praise God and worship Him without being entertained. Get together. Sing some songs. Share your victories and your sorrows. Read some Bible verses. Or just have a quiet evening reading together. Make it a sanctuary for harried city souls. You may find you have to expand your original meeting place!

Finally . . .

No matter what way you choose to celebrate the Sabbath, it can be a very special time of renewal and growth if you spend it with the One who created it. Share with others the great Sabbath joy you have found, and you will never lack for fellow "party-goers" as the sun sinks on Friday evening.

How to Create Your Own Special Sabbath Celebration

If you were going to throw a party tomorrow, what kind of party would you be likely to have? Would it be a big, rousing bash with one hundred of your closest friends? Or would it be a small, intimate affair with just family and maybe a best friend or two? Your choice says a lot about the kind of person you are, and it says a lot about what the word *celebration* means to you.

By nature I am an introvert. We're talking dedicated introvert here. I'm the kind of person who likes to be alone because I'm great company. I talk to myself. I even answer myself. There are people who say that talking to yourself means you have money in the bank. They are wrong.

The point remains that I'm a very shy, private person. It probably has a lot to do with the fact that I'm a writer and unless I'm alone I can't hear myself think, much less write. When I contemplate a celebration involving more than immediate family or close friends, it gives me hives.

So, I personally would go for the small, intimate party. We'd probably have some nice, quiet traditions; sensible, comfort food; and some deep spiritual insight. Maybe you'd like a whole gang singing Christian campfire songs. Or maybe you have no idea what you'd like to include in your Sabbath celebration.

That's what this chapter is all about. We'll work through some questions and try to determine what your celebrating style is and what particular elements of Sabbath celebration you would like to incorporate into your celebration. If possible, try to complete the following questions at one sitting to prevent interruptions to your train of thought.

My celebration style

What words do I associate with celebration?

_____ _____ _____

_____ _____ _____

_____ _____ _____

_____ _____ _____

At a celebration I am naturally: _____Talkative and social

_____Quiet and reserved

Of the traditions I've read about in this book, the ones I would most like to try are:_____

_____

_____

_____

Of the traditions listed, these could be instituted tomorrow without needing anything more than what I already have in my house:

_____

_____

Of the remaining traditions, I need these items before I can begin them. _____

_____

I would like to invite the following people to celebrate the Sabbath with me:

_____ _____ _____

_____ _____ _____

_____ _____ _____

_____ _____ _____

As a rule, I ___Like ___Dislike to cook and prepare for a celebration.

If "dislike," what convenience items could I use to make my celebration smoother and less stressful to prepare so that I could enjoy it more?_____

_____

Rate your daily prayer/Bible study on a scale of 1-10:_____

I could improve my daily prayer/Bible study by:_____

_____

_____

Which of the following things would you include in a Sabbath celebration? (circle all those that apply)

Singing   Praying   Sermonette   Special dinner
Discussion about spiritual matters
Religious music tapes or CDs   Candles   Devotional thought
Guests   Bible verses/memorization   Praise   Sabbath back rubs
Fresh flowers   Sparkling grape juice   Blessings Box
Special prayers   Blessing (for bread, children, etc.)
Sabbath table songs (zemirot)

Celebrating a Sabbath without company

Now, using the information above, let's map out a Sabbath celebration plan that you can use this coming Sabbath. Keep in mind that you should not include every single item that you would eventually like to have. Start with a few and build on that foundation.

Friday evening

Topic you have been reading about in your Bible study that you would like to discuss during the Sabbath hours: _____

_____

_____

Notes on this topic:

_____

_____

_____

How to Create Your Own Special Sabbath Celebration

Bible verse for this Sabbath:
_____

Devotional thought, Bible passage, or other spiritual message:
_____

Songs to sing/play: _____
_____

People to include in prayer:
_____
_____
_____
_____

New traditions to include: _____
_____
_____

What to have for dinner:
_____
_____

Sabbath

What time to get up: _____

What to read for a morning devotional time: _____
_____

MAKING SABBATH SPECIAL

What to have for breakfast: _____
_____

What I need to bring to church for any part I have in the service:
_____
_____

What to have for lunch: _____
_____

What to do after lunch (visit a nursing home, hospital, homebound member, take a walk): _____
_____

Closing Sabbath

Devotional thought: _____
_____

Bible passage for the coming week: _____

Songs to sing: _____
_____

People to pray for:
_____
_____
_____
_____

New traditions to include: _____

_____

_____

Inviting guests

Once you get the hang of celebrating, you will at some point probably play with the idea of having guests, be they many or be they few. Plan your Sabbath celebration ahead of time so you can concentrate on it rather than what you might have forgotten.

Sometime during the week invite your guests.
They are:

_____   _____

_____   _____

_____   _____

_____   _____

Friday evening

Topic you have been reading about in your Bible study that you would like to discuss during the Sabbath hours: _____

_____

Notes on this topic:

_____

_____

_____

_____

MAKING SABBATH SPECIAL

Particular questions about this topic to direct to specific guests:

Question:_____ Guest:_____
Question:_____ Guest:_____
Question:_____ Guest:_____

Bible verse for this Sabbath:

_____

Devotional thought, Bible passage, or other spiritual message:

_____

Songs to sing/play: _____

_____

People to include in prayer:

_____

_____

_____

_____

Traditions to include: _____

_____

_____

What to have for dinner:

_____

_____

How to Create Your Own Special Sabbath Celebration

Sabbath

What time to get up: _____

What to read for a morning devotional time: _____
_____

What to have for breakfast: _____
_____

What I need to bring to church for any part I have in the service:
_____
_____

What to have for lunch: _____
_____
_____

Who is coming to lunch:

_____   _____   _____

_____   _____   _____

_____   _____   _____

_____   _____   _____

What to do after lunch (visit a nursing home, hospital, homebound member, take a walk): _____
_____
_____

What guests should bring or part they should plan to be a part of:

Guest:_____ :_____

Guest:_____ :_____

Guest:_____ :_____

Guest:_____ :_____

Closing Sabbath

Devotional thought: _____

Presented by which guest: _____

Bible passage for the coming week: _____

Presented by which guest: _____

Songs to sing: _____

_____

People to pray for:

_____

_____

_____

_____

Traditions to include: _____

_____

_____

How to Create Your Own Special Sabbath Celebration

In the end it doesn't matter who you invite or what you do or which tradition you include in your celebration. What really matters is the joy in your heart when you open up and share these precious hours with the Creator of the universe. My friend Eric shared this quote with me, and I think it captures the wonder of Sabbath:

"God is so big He can cover the whole world with His love, and so small He can curl up inside your heart."—June Masters Bacher.

CHAPTER
8

Extra Special Touches

So, the Sabbath is coming, and you are ready to celebrate it. You're test driving some new traditions and liking them. There's a difference, and you can feel it. Sabbath is special, *cherished*. You are trying to accomplish your cooking before Sabbath, for Friday night and for Sabbath lunch. And there's the question of what to have.

What celebration would be complete without the food? Would you have a wedding without planning what to serve? Even a Super Bowl party depends to some extent on the food. The hoagie owes its existence to football. Yes, food is important.

The following is a collection of special recipes that work well together or separately. They are more than food; they are also an aesthetic feast. Preparation times are minimal. My life is such an extreme sport I can't make anything with a prep time of more than thirty minutes, so if *I* have time to make them, anyone does.

Don't throw up your hands in despair at the bread before you try making it. I used to think making bread was an all-day affair that would chain me to the kitchen. Then I took Mrs. Finley's cooking school, broadcast by satellite, to our church. Once I saw how easy it was, you couldn't stop me. Now I am a veritable bakery.

The breads in these recipes are the ones I make most often. They always get rave reviews. I mix, knead, and let the dough rise in the same bowl, so clean-up is a whiz. The actual time spent putting the ingredients together is no more than twenty minutes. The rest of the prep time is the rising and the baking.

If you used one sample menu for Friday's meal and one for Sabbath lunch, you would have enough meals for a month. Or try them for one Sabbath a month, and you'll have enough for four months; then start again.

Friday night

Menu: Lentil Spinach Stew
Focaccia bread

Lentil Spinach Stew

1 cup dry lentils
1 medium onion, chopped
3 cloves garlic, minced
1 Tbs. olive oil
4 cups water
4 tsp. McKay's chicken seasoning
1 Tbs. soy sauce

¼ tsp. salt
½ tsp. dried thyme, crushed
2 bay leaves
2 carrots, chopped
1 pkg. frozen, chopped spinach or 3 cups fresh chopped
1 Tbs. balsamic vinegar (optional)

Rinse the lentils and set them aside to drain. In a stockpot, cook the onion and garlic in the oil until tender but not browned. Stir in the remaining ingredients, except for the carrots and spinach and vinegar. Bring to a boil. Simmer for 20 minutes. Add carrots and spinach. Bring to a boil. Cover and simmer for 15 minutes or until the lentils are tender. Add vinegar if you are using it.

Focaccia Bread

4 ½ tsp. Yeast	2 tsp. salt
2 cups warm water	2 Tbs. fresh or 2 tsp. each dried
5 ½ cups unbleached white flour	rosemary and thyme
1 Tbs. sugar	½ cup sun-dried tomatoes
½ to 1 cup chopped	½ cup extra virgin olive oil
kalamata olives	

In a small bowl mix 4 ½ tsp. yeast (or 2 packages) with ½ cup warm water and 1 Tbs. sugar. Let it sit for about ten minutes until it gets foamy.

In the meantime, in a separate bowl mix:

5 ½ cups unbleached flour

2 tsp. salt

2 Tbs. chopped fresh or 2 tsp. dried of each: rosemary and thyme

To your bowl of yeast, add ½ to 1 cup of chopped kalamata olives (optional), ½ cup chopped sun-dried tomatoes (if using dried rather than oil-packed reconstitute before using in a small amount of warm water), ½ cup extra virgin olive oil, and 1 ½ cups of warm water. Mix well and add to dry ingredients, stirring well until thoroughly mixed.

Knead in the bowl (or if you prefer on a lightly floured countertop) just until the dough does not pull apart. As you knead, you will see it begin to stay in one ball and it will stop "ripping" as you turn it over to knead (*Note: If you are using the kalamata olives, the dough may continue to pull apart because of them*). Set it in a lightly oiled bowl with a cloth on top in a warm place to rise for 1 ½ hours.

Punch down the dough and preheat your oven to 450°F. Divide the dough in half and shape into two loaves. Press the dough out as if you were making a pizza crust. These will be freehand loaves, formed on cookie sheets. The loaf should be about the size of a dinner plate and about two inches thick. Don't worry if your loaf isn't two inches thick at first, because it is going to rise. It will look more like a deep dish pizza. Cover it and let the dough rise for 30 minutes.

Turn the oven down to 375°F. Dimple the dough with your finger-tips, brush it with olive oil, and sprinkle on coarse sea salt or Gorgonzola cheese or toasted and chopped pine nuts. Bake for 20-25 minutes or until golden brown.

Sabbath

Menu: Corn Olive Salad
Wholesome Whole-Wheat Crackers/Cheese

Corn Olive Salad

16-oz package frozen corn kernels
¼ cup black olives, chopped
¼ cup green olives, chopped
1 small onion, diced
½ tsp. dried dill
1 tsp. honey

1 medium green or red bell pepper
  cut into 1-inch strips
1 stalk celery, diced
1 Tbs. olive oil
3 Tbs. apple cider vinegar

Mix well and refrigerate until ready to serve.

Wholesome Whole-Wheat Crackers

2 cups regular oats
2 cups flour
  (mixture of rye, wheat, and white)
1 cup wheat germ
½ tsp. salt
¾ cup olive oil

2 cups quick oats
3 Tbs. sugar
garlic powder (to taste)
1 cup water

Mix dry ingredients well; then add the olive oil and water. If the mix is still too dry, add more water. Roll onto 2 large cookie sheets. If you line the pans first, cleanup is a snap. Sprinkle with salt. Cut into squares using a pizza cutter. Bake at 325° for 25-30 minutes. When they are brown at the edges, they are done. Watch them carefully; they will brown quickly when they start.

Serve with slices of cheese or a bean paste (mash any kind of bean and season with your favorite spices).

Friday night

Menu: Cabbage Crunch Salad
Bulgur Honey Wheat Rolls

Cabbage Crunch Salad

1 head cabbage, shredded
⅔ cups crumbled feta cheese
2 cups roasted sunflower seeds*

Mix well. Set aside.

*To roast sunflower seeds, place in dry pan on burner at medium heat. Stir constantly while they brown. When most of the seeds are brown, they are done.

Ginger Soy Sauce

2 large cloves garlic, minced
¼ cup soy sauce
½ cup olive oil
⅔ cup water

3 tsp. ginger
⅔ cup vinegar
¼ cup honey

Mix well and add to first mixture. Marinate for at least two hours in the refrigerator.

Bulgur Honey Wheat Rolls

1 cup bulgur
3 Tbs. butter or margarine
1 ½ cups boiling water
1 ¼ cups cold water
3 cups whole wheat flour
3 cups white flour

2 tsp. salt
⅓ cup molasses
1 Tbs. yeast
¾ cup warm water
¼ cup honey

In a bowl combine: bulgur, butter, and boiling water. Let this mixture stand for 30 minutes then stir in: cold water, salt, molasses, and honey.

In a separate bowl combine warm water and yeast. Let this stand for 5 minutes and then add it to the bulgur mixture. Stir in the whole-wheat flour and enough of the white flour so the dough can be handled. Turn out on a floured countertop or knead in the bowl until smooth and elastic. Place in greased bowl, turning to coat top of dough. Cover and let rise until double size (1-2 hours). Punch down and shape into rolls.

To fashion rolls: Pinch off a piece of dough about the size of lemon. Roll it between the flat of your hand and the countertop until it is a rope of dough about 6-8 inches long. With the ends facing away from you, put the right end over the left end, bring it under and up through the middle hole (as if you were going to tie a shoelace). Or shape each roll freehand and place on a cookie sheet.

Bake at 375°F for about 45 minutes until rolls are brown and sound hollow when tapped on the bottom.

Sabbath

Menu: Mushroom Barley Soup
Challah

Mushroom Barley Soup

1 ounce dried porcini (or Polish or shitake or button) mushrooms. Use fresh if you can't find dried.

10 cups water	1 ¼ cups onion, minced
1 ½ cups carrots, minced	1 cup celery, minced
1 ¼ cups pearl barley	Salt

Soak the dried mushrooms in 1 cup of boiling water for 45 minutes or until tender and reconstituted. In the meantime, put the water, onions, carrots, celery, and barley in a stockpot and bring to a boil. Reduce heat and simmer.

Strain the mushrooms using a sieve lined with paper towels (or use a coffee filter) and put the liquid in the pot. Remove the mushrooms, being careful not to take any grit or sand that might have been strained. Chop them and add to the pot.

Continue to simmer for about 45 minutes or until the barley is tender. Season with salt to taste.

Challah

Challah is the braided bread that is on every traditional Sabbath table. Observant Jewish cooks pinch off a piece of dough the size of an olive and burn it in the oven while the Challah bakes—and "oy vey," what a stench! This is called "taking challah" and symbolizes the tithe given to the priests at the time of the temple in Jerusalem. If you decide to burn the challah, turn off the smoke alarms first.

3 tsp. active dry yeast	7 to 8 cups white flour
1 ½ cups warm water	2 Tbs. sugar
8 cups flour	½ cup olive oil
3 medium eggs	Glaze: 1 egg yolk beaten with 1 Tbs. water

Mix yeast, ¼ cup of the water, and 1 tsp. of the sugar in a small bowl. Set aside until foamy. In a large bowl, mix the remaining sugar with the salt, oil, eggs, and 7 cups of the flour. Stir in the yeast mixture. Add the remaining water. Knead for five minutes. If the dough is sticky, add up to one cup more flour. It should be soft and supple but not sticky.

If you are kneading in the bowl, take the dough out and scrape any dried dough off the sides of the bowl. Oil it and return the dough, turning once to coat. Cover and set in a warm place to rise for 1 ½ - 2 hours. It will double in bulk. You can tell it's done by poking your finger in it. If the hole stays, it's risen enough. Punch it down, knead a couple times, and return it to the bowl (oil and turn again). Cover and let rise for 45 minutes.

Punch down again and divide the dough into six equal parts. Roll each piece into a rope about 12 inches long. They should be slightly fatter in the middle than on the ends. Line three of them up side by side (vertically to you). Pinch the tops together and begin to braid. Take the right rope and bring it over the middle rope. Then bring the left rope over the middle rope—just as if you were braiding hair. At the end of the braid, pinch the ends together to secure it.

The braiding should be snug. Don't leave any holes between the ropes. Repeat with the other three ropes. Place the loaves on a greased cookie sheet and cover them with towels. Let them rise again for 30 minutes. Heat the oven to 350°F. Before you put the loaves in the oven, brush the tops with the glaze. Bake for 30-45 minutes. When the loaves are done, they will be golden brown and sound hollow when you tap the bottoms.

Friday night

Menu: Hearty Pea Soup
Corn bread with honey butter

Hearty Pea Soup

1 medium sized onion	2 tsp. salt
1 Tbs. olive oil	1 medium carrot, chopped
1 bay leaf	3 stalks celery, chopped
1 tsp. celery seed	½ cup chopped parsley
2 tsp. miso (optional)	1 large potato, diced
1 cup green split peas	½ tsp. basil
¼ cup barley	½ tsp. thyme
2 quarts water	

Sauté the onion, with the bay leaf and celery seed in the oil until it is soft. Stir in peas, barley, and miso. Add the water and bring to a boil. Cook on low heat, partially covered, for 1 ½ hours.

Add remaining ingredients and lower the heat to a simmer. Cook for another 30-45 minutes. Thin with more water if desired. Adjust seasonings. Makes approximately 8 to 9 cups.

Corn Bread

1 cup white flour
¼ cup sugar
4 tsp. baking powder
½ tsp. Salt

1 cup cornmeal
2 eggs
1 cup milk (or tofu milk)
¼ cup olive oil

Mix dry ingredients. Add wet ingredients. Pour immediately into greased muffin tins or greased cake or bread pan. Bake at 425°F for 20-25 minutes.

Honey butter: Mix equal parts honey and butter. Melt in microwave until completely liquid. Drizzle over hot corn bread.

Sabbath

Menu: Rice Salad
Whole-Wheat Fruit Rolls

Rice Salad

5 cups rice, cooked
1 cup broccoli, chopped
1 cup carrots, grated
¾ cup sunflower seeds, roasted*
1 lb. tofu, fried in small amt. oil
½ cup feta cheese

Dressing:
1 cup olive oil
½ cup honey
¾ cup water
¾ cup vinegar

Mix dressing ingredients in large bowl. Add remaining ingredients and toss to coat well. Marinate for at least 2 hours before serving.

*To roast sunflower seeds, place in dry pan on burner at medium heat. Stir constantly while they brown. When most of the seeds are brown, they are done.

Whole-Wheat Fruit Rolls

3 tsp. active dry yeast
¼ cup warm water
2 ½ cups water
½ cup brown sugar
1 tsp. Salt

¼ cup light olive oil
½ cup wheat germ
3 cups whole wheat flour
4 cups unbleached white flour
1 cup oatmeal

Filling: 6 Tbs. melted butter, 6 Tbs. brown sugar, and 1 cup of mixed dried fruit (and nuts, optional). Cranberries, apricots, raisins, dates, and apples make great choices.

Mix yeast and warm water in small bowl. Set aside. In large bowl add water, brown sugar, salt, oil. Mix and then add wheat germ, flours, and oatmeal. Add yeast mixture. Knead (in bowl or on lightly floured surface) until satiny and smooth. Shape into a ball and place in oiled bowl, turning once to coat. Cover with a towel and let rise 1 ½ hours. Punch down.

Divide the dough into 3 equal pieces. Roll each piece out in a square about 16"x11". Brush with 2 Tbs. of the melted butter, sprinkle with 2 Tbs. of the brown sugar and 1/3 cup of the mixed fruit (and nuts). Beginning at the edge farthest away from you, roll the dough toward you as though you were rolling a jelly roll. Score the top with a knife every 2 inches. Repeat with remaining dough.

Cover and let rise for 1 hour. Bake at 350°F for 20-25 minutes.

Friday night

*Menu: Simple Vegetable Soup
Irish Soda Bread*

Simple Vegetable Soup

2 quarts water
1 tsp. miso
1 onion
2 carrots, diced
1 large potato, diced
3 cloves garlic, minced

2 stalks celery, diced
½ cup frozen corn
½ lb. tofu, diced and fried in small
    amount of oil untill brown.
½ frozen peas
1 Tbs. olive oil

In large stockpot heat water and miso. While it is heating, fry onion and garlic in oil for 2 to 3 minutes. Transfer to the stockpot and add remaining ingredients. Simmer for 1 hour or until vegetables are done.

Irish Soda Bread

3 cups whole-wheat flour
4 cups white flour
1 ¾ cups currants

1 tsp. salt
4 tsp. caraway seeds

Mix these together.

3 tsp. grated lemon peel
1 ⅓ cups buttermilk or tofu milk
⅔ cup light olive oil

1 cup cold water
3 Tbs. honey

Mix these together. Add to dry mixture and blend well.

Knead very briefly and shape the dough into two round loaves. Place on oiled cookie sheets, scoring the top to prevent cracking while baking. Bake at 350°F for about 45 minutes, until brown on top.

Sabbath

Menu: Hungarian Noodles
Apple Bran Muffins

Hungarian Noodles

10 dry oz. of flat, wide egg noodles
2 cloves garlic, minced
12 oz. cottage cheese
8 oz. sour cream
1 tsp. poppy seeds
salt to taste

¼ cup onions
1 Tbs. margarine or butter
1 tsp. vegetarian Worcestershire
sauce or soy sauce
paprika

Cook the noodles until they are done. Drain them. While they are draining, sauté the onions and garlic in margarine. When the onions are translucent, add to noodles with the remaining ingredients (except paprika). Pour into a baking dish and sprinkle with paprika. Bake at 375°F for 1 hour.

Apple Bran Muffins

1 cup whole wheat flour
¾ cup wheat bran
¼ tsp. salt
½ tsp. baking soda
½ tsp. freshly grated nutmeg
2 tsp. grated orange rind
1 egg
¼ cup molasses

¼ cup raisins
¼ cup chopped walnuts
juice of ½ orange
1 cup buttermilk or sour milk or
soured tofu milk(to sour add 1 to
2 tsp. lemon juice)
1 medium apple, grated
1 Tbs. light olive oil

Preheat oven to 350°F. In a large bowl, mix flour, bran, salt, soda, and nutmeg. Add the orange rind, apples, raisins, and walnuts. In a separate bowl, mix the orange juice, buttermilk (or soured tofu milk), egg, molasses, and oil. Stir the liquid ingredients into the dry ones, using as few strokes as possible. Mix only until incorporated. Pour into greased muffin tins and bake for 25 minutes. Makes 12 regular muffins. These are even better the next day.

CHAPTER
9

And Finally, Brethren . . .

At the beginning of this book, I started by telling you what Sabbath was like around my house. This book has been a journey as much for me as for you. Our Sabbath experience has been enriched by the material I have uncovered about Sabbath and by the fellowship with the people at The Community who have such an abundant blessing of the Holy Spirit in their lives. They have been a wonderful testimony of singleminded living for God.

When people ask me what I'm working on these days and I tell them about this book, the subject of The Community always comes up. And they are always more interested in what The Community believes and how their doctrine differs from ours than in what they live. *And yet how we live is what really matters.*

Yes, having the whole truth is really important. But living the truth you have is even more important. And until we do that, we can celebrate the Sabbath every week with all the enthusiasm of ringing in the New Year, and it isn't going to make any difference in our lives because it will still be just a form, works with no faith and no love.

Other Adventists have been very guarded about my associations with The Community. Afraid, I suppose, that some of it might rub off. I hope it does! I wish I could be as Nahara, who told me about how difficult it is living as a community at times. You would think their families spend a lot of time together, but Nahara's family lives at the second house, not near the soap shop where her husband works during the day. He is gone all day and then when he gets back, there might be meetings, or someone will want to talk with him about something. She and the kids don't get to see him very often sometimes.

I've been in that situation before. My reaction is to complain. Bitterly. Nahara's reaction? She prays for grace to be able to patiently bear her burdens, to love the people she lives with, and to put their concerns over her own. She knows that Yahshua is a bottomless well of grace and strength and all she has to do is go to Him and ask for more. That is not her last-ditch-when-all-else-fails effort, it is her first thought!

Ouch!

I find it hard to believe Jesus could come back and say to people who really love Him, but have interpreted the Bible wrongly, "I'm so sorry. You love Me, I can see that. But, wow, were you ever way off in your interpretation of last-day events. I'm afraid your names aren't in the Book of Life. Next, please."

We have so much light on many biblical topics. But this doesn't make us superior, just more *responsible*. We can take the brilliant light we have and hide it under a bushel basket of apathy, utterly failing to communicate it to the world as God asked us to. Can we then say that it's the world's fault that they are ignorant of what we were supposed to tell them? No, it's ours because we didn't shout our message from the rooftops to everyone, not just those who have it all together and are presentable enough to tolerate in our pews each week.

Having greater light is a great source of pride to us. It's given us a hearty case of—as my friend Jen puts it—self-righteousnessitis. But the greater the light, the greater is the responsibility to shine. One aspect of our life that should shine the brightest is the Sabbath. If it is dry and formalistic, people are not going to see our compassionate, life-saving, and awesome God!

I don't know about you, but I'm ready to go home. The longer I am here, the more my heart groans for Jesus to come back for us. I don't want to wait any longer, and I know what's holding us up. It's us. Jesus is ready to come back. But we're not.

These are the LAST DAYS! We need to shake off any remaining chains securing us to this world, gather our loved ones together with us, and prepare to check out of this dark, gloomy, horrible place. Jesus is coming for us! Get ready!

> The heavens will disappear with a roar; the elements will be destroyed by fire, and the earth and everything in it will be laid bare. Since everything will be destroyed in this way, what kind of people ought you to be? You ought to live holy and godly lives as you look forward to the day of God and *speed its coming*. That day will bring about the destruction of the heavens by fire, and the elements will melt in the heat. But in keeping with his promise we are looking forward to a new heaven and a new earth, *the home of righteousness* (2 Peter 3:10-13, emphasis mine).

Let's GO already!

And I can hear you saying, "But I've tried. It's not my fault. It's my family or my church or my relatives or my pets . . ." It's always something, someone else. But the buck's got to stop here. Renewal and revival have to start somewhere, with someone. Let that someone be you.

OK, maybe your complaints are valid. Maybe your family is unsaved or won't participate in a deeper spiritual experience. That certainly can drag you down. Maybe it's your relatives who constantly badger and persecute you for your faith. Or your church is dead or worse, gone off the deep end one way or another.

But none of that has to stop YOU. Because a relationship with Jesus takes place on a person-to-person basis. Jesus worked with the disciples one on one. He didn't have a collective relationship with them. If that had happened, then Judas would have thrown the whole thing off. Each of the disciples developed a relationship with Him personally.

And they didn't all develop at the same time. That's why you only see John at the foot of the cross. Determine to be a John today, and don't worry about Peter and James and Judas and the rest of them. Just concentrate on being the best John you can be.

Sabbath at my house is changing. We're trying out some of the new traditions I have discovered during the course of writing this book. Someday, I hope to get a shofar to blow at the beginning of Sabbath, but for now that's just a dream. But the most important change is inside us.

We turn more easily to God these days, and we rely on Him more. That's not something that always comes easily, but it is something the weekly celebration of Sabbath reminds us of every time it draws near. If the week has been too busy or we've pulled away from God, we are reminded by the Sabbath that He is there, just waiting to free us from the unreasonable burdens we heap onto ourselves.

The Sabbath is a celebration, but it is also a time to let God renew our hearts and our minds. It's time to set our priorities straight for the coming week. And we have that opportunity each Sabbath. We can confess that we've strayed and ask God to help us to stay close to Him throughout each day of the coming week. And the next Sabbath is only six days away.

It is my prayer for you as this Sabbath approaches that you will find a wonder and a delight in it that you have never seen before. May it fill you so full of the Holy Spirit that you will overflow and shower blessings on all those around you.

Shabbat shalom!